QUESTIONS
COUPLES
ASK

Resources by Les and Leslie Parrott

Books
Becoming Soul Mates
Getting Ready for the Wedding
The Love List
Love Is
The Marriage Mentor Manual
Meditations on Proverbs for Couples
Questions Couples Ask
Relationships
Relationships Workbook
Saving Your Marriage Before It Starts
Saving Your Marriage Before It Starts Workbook for Men
Saving Your Marriage Before It Starts Workbook for Women
Saving Your Second Marriage Before It Starts
Saving Your Second Marriage Before It Starts Workbook for Men
Saving Your Second Marriage Before It Starts Workbook for Women
When Bad Things Happen to Good Marriages
When Bad Things Happen to Good Marriages Workbook for Men
When Bad Things Happen to Good Marriages Workbook for Women

Video Curriculum—Zondervan *Groupware*™
Relationships
Saving Your Marriage Before It Starts
Mentoring Engaged and Newlywed Couples

Audio Pages®
Relationships
Saving Your Marriage Before It Starts
Saving Your Second Marriage Before It Starts
When Bad Things Happen to Good Marriages

Books by Les Parrott III
Control Freak
Helping Your Struggling Teenager
High Maintenance Relationships
The Life You Want Your Kids to Live
Seven Secrets of a Healthy Dating Relationship
Once Upon a Family

Books by Leslie Parrott
If You Ever Needed Friends, It's Now
God Loves You Nose to Toes (children's book)

QUESTIONS
COUPLES
ASK

ANSWERS TO THE TOP 100 MARITAL QUESTIONS

DR. LES PARROTT III
& DR. LESLIE PARROTT

ZONDERVAN™

GRAND RAPIDS, MICHIGAN 49530 USA

ZONDERVAN™

Questions Couples Ask
Copyright © 1996 by Les and Leslie Parrott

Requests for information should be addressed to:

Zondervan, *Grand Rapids, Michigan 49530*

Library of Congress Cataloging-in-Publication Data

Parrott, Les.
    Questions Couples Ask: Answers to the Top 100 Marital Questions/ Les Parrott III
and Leslie Parrott.
        p. cm.
    Includes bibliographical references and index
    ISBN: 0-310-20754-1 (softcover)
    1. Marriage—Miscellanea. 2. Marriage—Religious aspects—Christianity. I.
Parrott, Leslie L., 1964 – . II Title.
HQ734.P219 1996
306.81-dc 20   96-25962
                                                                                            CIP

Interior design by Sue Vandenberg Koppenol

Printed in the United States of America

07 08 09 10 /❖DC/ 20 19 18

To Dennis and Lucy Guernsey
Marriage mentors who have answered
countless questions without speaking a word

CONTENTS

ACKNOWLEDGMENTS

Thanks . . .

To our friend Norm Wright for suggesting to us that marriage mentors and newlyweds have a need for a book like this. We would have never attempted it without his kind prompting.

To Tad Beckwith and Laurie Nouguier for their invaluable assistance in tracking down information for this project, often at a moment's notice.

To Sandy Vander Zicht and Lori Walburg for their editorial savvy and personal kindness during the writing of this project. Superb, as always.

To Scott Bolinder for sharing our dream to equip married couples with the most effective tools possible and for helping to make the dream a reality.

To the hundreds of couples we have seen in counseling and the thousands who have participated in our marriage seminars. You asked the questions contained in this book, and your quest for knowledge was our inspiration.

HOW NEWLYWEDS
CAN USE THIS BOOK

"Man will not live without answers to his questions," said American diplomat Hans J. Morgenthau. He might just as well have said, "Newlyweds will not survive without answers to their questions."

It's true. Every new couple comes to marriage with an unrealized set of questions to be answered, and the success of their marriage hinges on finding the information that can answer those questions. We have counseled hundreds of newlyweds who confess that they didn't even know what questions to ask until after they got married. That's normal. The emotional high of planning an exciting wedding celebration temporarily takes a couple's eyes off the marriage itself. But once you have had a chance to settle into married life, new questions about making your relationship the best it can be begin to emerge on a regular basis: How do we keep romance alive? What can we do if our sex drives differ? Should we ever keep secrets from each other? What if our in-laws smother us? and on and on.

This book is designed to help you get your questions answered quickly and succinctly. The format allows you to readily target your topic and, in just a few pages, read some practical information about it. The book is not designed to be read clear through. Rather, it is a handy reference for you to use when a question arises.

In the last few years we have been taking note of what newlyweds are asking in the first few years of marriage, and we have attempted to include their most common questions in this book. We organized them into twelve categories that include communication, conflict, careers, emotions, money, sex, in-laws, and so on. By looking through the table of contents and using the book's index, you can pinpoint the area where you need advice. In addition, each category concludes with a few recommendations of other books on the topic that you may want to check out.

We did not write this book to be comprehensive or to be the final answer on any topic. It is simply a starting place, a jumping-off spot for discussion between partners as well as a place for finding additional helpful information.

Philosopher Francis Bacon once said, "A prudent question is one-half of wisdom." We agree. And the other half is finding the answer to that question. We hope this book helps you do just that.

How Marriage Mentors Can Use This Book

We've all heard the frightful statistics on marital failure these days—some of us to the point of growing numb. But what still shocks people is that in the face of risky odds, the majority of new couples are getting little if any serious preparation to keep their lifelong commitment and build a happy marriage. In fact, less than a fifth of all marriages in America are preceded by some kind of formal marriage preparation.

What does this mean? Among other things, it means that most newly married couples come into marriage with dozens of unanswered questions. It also means that these couples often don't even know the questions to ask until after they get married. That's where you come in.

Over the last several years we have coordinated something we call the "Marriage Mentor Club." Every couple that comes through our marriage preparation program in Seattle is linked with a mature, healthy couple who has committed to walk with them through their first year. We have described this program in detail in our book *The Marriage Mentor Manual* (Zondervan). In short, the mentoring consists of three meetings with the couple where they can have an opportunity to discuss issues and ask questions of an objective, experienced couple. Churches and other organizations around the country are doing the same thing. In fact, marriage mentoring is turning out to be one of the most effective methods of helping new couples build a love that goes the distance.

One of the most rewarding aspects of these mentoring programs is not only the help they give new couples but the benefits they bring to the mentor couples themselves. Almost always, after investing in a new couple for a year, mentors ask for another couple to help because of the good it has done for their own marriage. The only real complaint we ever hear from mentors is that they lack the resources to help their couples with all of their concerns. "We don't have a personal library of marriage books," one mentor couple told us, "and since we sometimes don't have the answers to the questions couples ask, we're not sure where to turn." Others have told us that they could go to a public library or a bookstore to hunt for a resource that might help, but, understandably, they rarely took the time for this.

It was this concern from marriage mentors that prompted us to write this book. We wanted to provide a resource that brought together the most commonly asked questions by newlyweds and put the answers between the covers of one book.

As a mentor couple, you can use this book as a reference tool to help your mentorees find the answers they seek. The various categories and the book's index can help you quickly pinpoint the issues you are trying to learn more about. Also, each category concludes with a brief listing of some of the most helpful books we know of on particular issues. You can read through the annotations to find an additional resource if you feel it would be helpful. In this way, *Questions Couples Ask* will serve as a springboard to help you gather what you need to be the most effective mentor couple possible.

It may seem superficial to say so here, but we sincerely thank you for taking the time and energy to invest in the next generation of married couples. As mentors, you are giving a lifelong gift to newlyweds that just might make a world of difference in their lives.

CHAPTER ONE:

QUESTIONS ABOUT COMMUNICATION

My wife says that listening is the most important part of good communication in marriage. Do you agree? And if so, why is what we hear more important than what we say in our conversations?

You are fortunate to have such a wise wife. Listening was (and probably still is) one of my biggest communication struggles with Leslie. Like your wife, she seemed to understand the importance of this skill better than I did. For me, communication was all about trying to get my point across, not so much about trying to understand my wife's perspective through hearing what she had to say. I have since come to respect why your wife and mine put so much emphasis on listening—it solves many, if not most, of the communication problems in marriage. In fact, we often tell couples that almost all of their conflictual conversation could be resolved if each partner would seek to understand before being understood—in other words, if each would learn to listen.

Listening is basic to learning. In fact, listening consumes more time than reading, speaking, and writing combined.[1] When you consider this fact, it should not come as a surprise to realize that good listening is a "must" for every successful marriage.

Every spouse who feels cherished by his or her mate will tell you that they feel taken care of primarily because their spouse listens to them. Listening is love in action. Nowhere is it more appropriate than in marriage, yet many couples never truly listen to each other.

Listening is a sign of affirmation. When spouses truly listen, they contribute to one another's self-esteem. When they don't, the interpretation is frequently negative. Be honest. How do you feel when you sense that your spouse is not listening to you? Without being listened to, feelings of rejection are almost inevitable.

Listening requires you to set aside preconceived ideas or judgments and convey a message of acceptance of the person. In fact, listening does not necessarily convey an acceptance of the message, but it does convey an acceptance of the messenger. Think about it. When you are listened to, genuinely listened to, you feel that your spouse is someone with whom you can be fully known and share all of your inner thoughts, weaknesses, and foibles—because he or she accepts you.

Listening opens up another's spirit. When your spouse is speaking and you are not preoccupied or distracted, you are, in effect, saying, "You are very important to me, and I am interested in you." This taps into your partner's deepest need to be understood, and in return he or she will open up all the more.

Nearly every couple we talk to says that communication is the key to a successful marriage. But when we ask these same couples what "good communication" is, we get a lot of foggy answers. Can you pinpoint the most essential parts of good communication for us?

"If you were to boil down good communication skills to their bare essence," we are sometimes asked, "what would you have?" With so many thick books on communication, it is sometimes difficult to cut through the clutter and sum it all up. The following is our attempt:

1. *Send clear and accurate messages.* Precise and unambiguous statements facilitate good communication, while imprecise and ambiguous statements hinder it. Consider the difference between these two statements: "You hurt me tonight at the party" versus "I was hurt when you spent almost all of your time at the party watching television instead of talking with our friends."

2. *Avoid incongruent messages.* Do not send simultaneous messages with mutually exclusive meanings. How many messages are contained in the following statements? "There is nothing wrong! And I don't want to talk about it!" Most often, incongruent messages come from a statement that is not in sync with the person's facial expression or tone of voice. When a husband says, "I'm happy to wait for you," but his tone and posture indicate that he is definitely not happy to do so, he is sending an incongruent message that is destined to cause a communication breakdown.

3. *Be empathic.* Empathy can be defined as listening with your heart as well as your head to truly understand what your spouse is thinking, feeling, and experiencing. Empathy involves putting yourself in your partner's shoes and imagining what life would be like from his or her perspective. When your partner tells you about feeling rejected by someone at work, for example, put yourself in his or her position. Use your heart to imagine how you would feel if rejected. Then use your head to accurately understand if what you would be feeling is the same as what your partner is feeling. Every time you empathize, you better understand what your spouse is saying.

4. *Provide feedback.* Communication involves an exchange of information. The response (or feedback) to the message the other person has sent indicates the message was (or was not) received and was (or was not) understood. "Yes, go on, I'm listening." "No, I don't understand that. Please repeat it." Providing these kinds of simple statements, as well as being attentive

with your eyes and body posture, lets your spouse know he or she is being understood—that you are genuinely interested in hearing the message.

5. *Be generous with supportive and positive statements.* Accuracy, empathy, and feedback are all important. But we all like to feel good about ourselves. When we give recognition to our spouses, when we compliment their accomplishments, and when we reassure them of how important they are to us, we not only make them feel better, we build a stronger foundation for communication. When we feel supported and are supportive, many of the other basic communication skills fall more naturally into place.

While there are plenty of additional elements to good communication, these five qualities are some that we view as being most important. In fact, you might want to review this list from time to time and think about your own communication style. Ask yourself how often you use the practices listed here with your spouse.

It helps to have good communication skills boiled down to the basics, but knowing what we should be doing and actually doing it are two different stories. Do you have any tips on putting these skills into practice?

You are so right. This may sound strange, but we have discovered that talking about good communication is often easier than practicing it. Too often, we understand what to do but for a variety of reasons—we're distracted, feeling stressed out, or simply forgetting what to do—we don't do it. Even the experts sometimes have difficulty following their own advice. I know we do. Not long ago, on a flight from Denver to Seattle, we found ourselves in the middle of a complete communication breakdown. We were returning home after speaking all weekend to couples at a marriage seminar. Can you believe it? We knew what to do to get out of our dilemma, but neither one of us was doing it. So we finally resorted to a strategy we developed quite some time ago.

After years of trying to practice good communication, we have found it helpful to sometimes use a "cheat sheet." A small card or piece of paper carried in a purse or wallet can contain three or four basic communication reminders to keep us on track. When we find our conversation breaking down, pulling out this little card tells us what we need to do to correct the problem. It's amazing how helpful a simple device like this can be. Our cheat sheet, for example, says: "Seek to understand before being understood. Clarify what you hear. Use 'I' statements instead of 'you' statements. Focus on feelings and not just content."

Something else that has helped is what we call "micro-communication skills." If you have ever taken golf lessons, you know that the instructor begins by having you focus on only one skill at a time. The first lesson, for example, may be solely on how you hold the club. You will hit dozens of balls while focusing solely on your grip. Next, the position of your feet is the focal point, then your shoulders, and so on. The same is true of learning good communication. Try focusing on just one skill at a time. In your next conversation, for example, be empathic. Use your head and your heart to put yourself in your partner's shoes. Don't worry about any of the other important skills. Just think about what your partner is experiencing. By limiting yourself in this way, you will better put into practice all of what you need to have good communication—one skill at a time.

If you continue to experience frustration in not being able to practice what you know to do, seek some coaching. An objective third party, such as a counselor, can often help you see your blind spots and transcend them. In only a session or two, you will most likely find your communication taking huge strides forward.

When we were dating, we could finish each other's sentences. Now that we are married, it seems I don't know what is going on in his head most of the time. What happened?

In a general sense, women want to relate and talk about feelings, while husbands want to address issues and offer solutions. This pattern, barely evident during the dating years, becomes increasingly blatant after the wedding. So if you are feeling as if you don't "understand" one another the way you used to, don't despair. You simply need to learn the art of communicating as a married couple.

The lesson begins by recognizing your various levels of conversation. Robert and Rosemary Barnes explain that once a couple gets married they tend to talk on three different levels.[2] To have a growing and fulfilling marriage where both partners feel understood, a couple needs to move to "Level Three."

But let's start with "Level One." This is the most shallow level of communication, what the Barneses call the Grunt Level. It involves an obligatory response: "Hello," "How ya doing?" Words are exchanged at this level, but the communication is far from deep. Unfortunately, many couples approach each other at this level. They get home from work and "talk" a bit about their day, but neither person really listens.

"Level Two" is just a step above the grunt level of communicating. It is the Journalist Level, where talking with one's spouse involves expressing opinions, but only on mundane facts. The conversation involves politics, other people, the church, but it stops there. Nothing is said about each other's feelings. That's reserved for the next level.

"Level Three" is the Feelings Level. Spouses reach this level when they feel safe enough to share areas of weakness or feelings that may put them in a bad light. This is a vulnerable step involving opening up one's spirit and allowing your partner to see the real you. This is the only level on which real understanding occurs.

Whenever we talk to couples in our counseling office about these three levels, they quickly want to know what they can do to create the kind of safety where both of them are willing to risk communicating at the third level. You are probably wondering the same thing for your marriage. Well, the answer is really quite simple in principle, but more difficult in practice. It is to listen for each other's feelings and reflect them back. Underneath every message your spouse communicates is a river of emotions that you can tap into. Don't look for these feelings to be clearly labeled—they aren't. The signs are subtle, hidden beneath the verbiage and the body language. Your spouse may not say, "I'm frustrated," for example, but he or she might reveal this in tone or demeanor. When this is the case, you can say, "It sounds like you are frustrated." A simple statement like this is all that is needed to bring Level Two conversation to Level Three—the place where genuine understanding takes place.

Jenny and Ron, a couple starting their second year of marriage, came to us because of an excruciating breakdown in communication. "We used to have long talks before we got married," Jenny confessed. "Now we barely say good morning." After just one hour of practicing this simple skill of reflecting each other's feelings, Jenny and Ron could notice a difference. They didn't have it down pat after just one session, but they knew what they needed to do to restore their conversations to a feelings level. This gave them hope, and after a couple weeks of practice, both of them gave us the same report: "We understand each other better than we ever have before."

I have tried reflecting my partner's feelings and it feels so phony, like I'm a robot or something. Is there any way to do this without feeling as though you are just using a technique?

We hear this question a lot. Sometimes in one of our seminars we will teach this technique of reflecting each other's feelings and then have couples practice it right then and there. Invariably someone will raise their hand and echo your same frustration. Our answer is always the same: Reflecting your partner's feelings will remain an empty technique and fall flat on its face unless you are genuinely interested in understanding your partner.

As long as you are sincere about your desire to know your partner's heart, reflecting his or her feelings will work like a charm. You may feel awkward at first. Yes, you may even feel like a robot programmed to say, "It sounds as though you are feeling . . ." But if you practice this routinely for a week or so, and if you are genuinely wanting to make a deep connection with your spouse, you will see just how natural it can become.

By the way, you don't have to always begin your reflection with "It sounds like . . ." Here are some additional leads that may be helpful:

> *It seems as if . . .*
> *What I hear you saying is . . .*
> *It must have been . . .*
> *Could it be that you are feeling . . .*
> *You must feel . . .*
> *I wonder if you are feeling . . .*

Even using a variety of leads to reflect your partner's feelings may still feel a bit phony, but don't give up. It is natural to feel awkward anytime we try something new. Keep at it. In a relatively brief amount of time, with enough practice, you will begin to reflect feelings with a natural ease that becomes part of your daily conversations.

One more thing. You don't have to be a "feelings" expert to decipher your partner's emotions. The good news is that when you are genuinely interested in understanding his or her heart, you can reflect back a feeling that isn't really on target and still succeed with this practice. Your partner may be feeling frustrated and you say, from a genuine heart, "It sounds as if you are feeling pretty angry." Your partner may not be feeling angry at all, but because you are genuinely interested in understanding her, she will not shut down. Instead, she will say something like, "Well, I'm not really angry as much as I am just plain frustrated." Do you see how it works? Even when you are wrong, this technique works—as long as you are genuine.

So if you listen carefully to your partner, you will hear many different feelings. You will "hear" them in their eyes, in their fidgeting, even in their silence. Think of this kind of listening as mining for feelings. Once you think you have identified a potential feeling, check it out with your partner. You will be surprised how understood they feel.

It seems like the communication experts put a lot of emphasis not only on listening but also on nonverbal communication. Why is nonverbal communication so important in marriage?

What we say to each other is only part of the communication process. How we say it—with a smile, or a shrug, or a frown, or a glare—is at least as important, sometimes more. Some communication experts say that as much as ninety percent of our communication is nonverbal.[3] Whether you like it or not, you are saying a great deal more with your body than you are with your words. Consider eye contact. Whether or not you are maintaining eye contact reveals how genuinely interested you are in understanding your spouse. But not only do good conversationalists do a lot of eye-to-eye gazing, scientists have found that their pupils actually dilate, an involuntary response indicating pleasure at what they see. Amazing, isn't it? Your eyes really are the window to your soul. By the way, you can't fake the size of your pupil dilation. Either you're genuinely interested or you're not; your eyes won't lie.

Eye contact isn't the only nonverbal clue to a couple's relationship. Unhappy couples, according to John Gottman, exhibit a wide array of gestures and body language that give away their estrangement.[4] They lean away from each other; there's lots of rolling of eyes and crossing of arms and more rigidness. Gottman's research shows that women who are unhappy often unconsciously roll back their upper lip while they talk. And both men and women who are contemptuous of their spouse will tilt their head back and literally look down their nose at their spouse, as if sniffing something unpleasant.

Loving couples, on the other hand, often touch each other while they talk, and that doesn't necessarily mean something as conventional as holding hands. A pat on the forearm, brushing a stray thread off a lapel, or even intertwining feet are tender ways of intensifying the verbal connection. These couples also lean close to each other, as if a magnet were at work.

The bottom line on nonverbal communication? If you are relying on words alone to communicate to each other, you are fooling yourselves. Research has found that husbands and wives are quite accurate interpreters of their spouses' nonverbal communication. In fact, husbands whose wives send clear messages through facial expressions reported fewer complaints in the marriage.[5] Nonverbal communication is critically important to helping you understand and be understood.

Sometimes when I bring up a topic that is important to me, my spouse will say, "This is a bad time." Is his reaction just a defense, or is there truly a "right" time to say certain things?

You have probably heard that the best way to solve relationship problems is to talk about them. But while that is often true, there is also wisdom in not talking—in biding your time, walking away, or simply keeping quiet and getting on with things.

Your spouse plops down at the kitchen table and proposes a summer vacation camping trip that includes backpacking and white-water rafting. You hate camping and, besides, you had your heart set on a trip to visit your family. What do you do? If you are like most married people, you burst into a tirade accusing your partner of not considering what you want.

It is during these times that you can save yourself and your marriage a lot of wear and tear by practicing a little silence. You see, the best time to talk about problems or ideas may not be when they occur to you, but later, after you've put some perspective on the issue. Rather than burst forth with your feelings, it is better to put some perspective on the issue by giving it some time.

Management consultants in the workplace teach their clients the principle of "power stalling." The idea is to respond to new ideas by saying: "That's interesting. Let me think about it, and I'll get back to you." This same tactic can work at home. When your partner runs an idea by you, don't scream and say you don't like it; instead, say, "Let me think about it." This buys you a cooling-off period and gives you time to weigh how you really feel about something without the pressure of having to give a spontaneous response.

The same principle applies when you are the one with the idea or comment. Give yourself time to plan how to package it, how to present it, and the best time to say it. You might even schedule some time by saying to your partner, "Let's go out for breakfast on Saturday. I have something I really want to talk to you about." The idea is to talk so your spouse will listen.

Another tip for saying the right thing at the right time is to be sure both of you are acting rationally. Say you want to discuss working out a more equitable arrangement regarding the laundry, and your partner starts screeching that you are always criticizing him or her. That's when it's time to back down and discuss the laundry issue later. You can say, "Let's talk about this when we are both a little saner."

If you are feeling out of control of your feelings, of course, this is another time to leave things unsaid. Don't believe the myth that says it is always best to get things off your chest. It isn't. If you are in the grip of anger, you are bound to say things you will later regret.

One more thing about finding the "right" time to say something: Don't mistake sexual intimacy for an open invitation to talk about an unrelated issue that's bothering you. Resist, for instance, the urge to use post-lovemaking euphoria as an opportunity to discuss your money fears. Women sometimes think that since their husbands are being physically intimate they'll talk intimately. But men are much more compartmentalized—to most men, sex is sex and talk is talk. So be sure you are accurately reading your partner's mood before you launch into a major talk. And remember that silence is not only golden but sometimes vital to your marriage.

Most of the time, I am up-front and honest with my partner, but when I have some bad news or any kind of information she won't like to hear, I'm not sure how to communicate it. How can I be honest without hurting my partner's feelings?

Whether you have read the old best-selling book or not, you were probably taught the "I'm okay—you're okay" philosophy of accepting others as they are. There's a lot of truth to it. People *are* healthier when in an accepting, nonjudgmental environment. But, on the other hand, there are times in marriage when you need to point out a personal quirk or flaw, a blind spot, that could hurt your partner. After all, it can be disastrous to a marriage not to help each other become more self-aware, grow, and change. Pointing out how a partner was insensitive to somebody, for example, helps him or her become more sensitive, more healthy, and thus a better marriage partner. Without honest feedback, marriages would be doomed to stagnation and emptiness.

Giving honest input to your partner, however, is trickier than you might guess. A fundamental principle required for honest feedback is to recognize that you need honest feedback too. You need to be open to and even invite your partner to serve as a mirror to you, reflecting back the truth of how you really are. This lays the groundwork for a process of "mutual education" in which each partner helps the other person grow. At the heart of mutual education is the principle of gentle persuasion, not coercion. The message of mutual education is "I love you; I believe this information will benefit you and our marriage."

So the key to giving honest input without hurting your spouse is to agree that both of you, for the sake of each other and your marriage, will invite honest feedback and lovingly provide it.

Once you reach this agreement, stay clear of several danger spots in giving honest input to your partner. Overgeneralizing, for example, is always a no-no. "You always think it's my fault" is a gross exaggeration. Words like *always* or *never* cannot characterize the situation accurately. It is much better to say, "Sometimes when we argue I get the feeling that it's my fault."

Also, avoid commands: "Stop putting your elbows on the table." Instead, say, "People might get the wrong impression when they watch you at the table. Could I make a suggestion?" The point is to avoid criticism or nagging.

When you are giving honest feedback in marriage, you can think of yourselves as a pair of mountain climbers, each lending a hand to the other, each making suggestions and encouraging the other, as you work together toward becoming healthier individuals and building a rock-solid marriage.

My partner accuses me of keeping him in the dark, of not telling him everything. I, on the other hand, believe we should respect one another's privacy on some matters. What do you think? Should we never keep a secret from each other?

Most of us were raised to believe that in good marriages, there are no secrets—that couples should tell each other *everything*. We believe that in a good marriage spouses are totally transparent with each other, revealing all of what they think, feel, and do so that absolutely nothing is hidden. But while this ideal may seem to make sense on the surface, the truth is that your marriage can only take so much honesty. Some things are better left unsaid. Without a healthy sense of privacy and censored self-disclosure, your marriage will become more like a battlefield than a safe haven.

The trick is to find a balance of openness and privacy that works best for you as a couple. That's why we recommend that you begin this process by exploring your different expectations about privacy and openness. Most couples have tacit ideas about what their spouse should tell them, but discussing them explicitly can be very revealing.

After you take time to understand each other's expectations, you might want to agree upon some guidelines to keep you connected while still respecting your privacy. For example, our rule of thumb is that if something's going to affect the two of us, we talk about it (e.g., a change at work that will affect the stress level in our home). We don't want any disconcerting surprises. However, we don't believe there's any reason to go into tremendous detail about something that doesn't have a direct impact on our marriage (e.g., the particulars of personnel restructuring at work).

When it comes to revealing details about every feeling one experiences, we have also learned to think before we speak. Why? Because some thoughts and feelings are only transitory. They last for a few moments and are gone. So if you have a fleeting feeling about quitting your job, for example, you don't have to tell your spouse about it if you know it would cause unnecessary anxiety. Along these same lines, total transparency can lead to saying hurtful things. We need to consider whether what we say is the product of an "unbridled tongue" or of "speaking the truth in love." In the New Testament, James suggests the tongue should be a monitor rather than an open channel of our thoughts (James 1:26).

Of course some things must be told, no matter how painful. We have counseled some people who have kept significant information from their partner because they didn't want to hurt them. For example, one man had been fired and had invested joint funds in racehorses and never said a word about it because it seemed easier not to have to contend with his wife's reaction. We have known of a situation where the wife didn't find out that her husband had high blood pressure until she found an empty medication vial in the bathroom wastebasket, months after his initial diagnosis. In the long term, keeping these kinds of secrets will damage any trust between two people dedicated to each other.

A common pattern of secrecy that can undermine your marriage is routinely sneaking around buying things and hiding them from the other person. Afraid of being scolded, the buyer feeds into outmoded roles in which the other spouse serves as the "parent" controlling the purse strings.

To maintain a balance between openness and privacy, you have to steer clear of deception. While you aren't obligated to tell your spouse everything, you will build a stronger marriage by speaking the truth in love.

What are some of the most helpful resources on communication in marriage?

Men Are from Mars, Women Are from Venus: A Practical Guide for Improving Communication and Getting What You Want in Your Relationships by John Gray (HarperCollins, 1992).

Using the metaphor of Martians and Venusians attempting to communicate, John Gray illustrates commonly occurring conflicts between men and women when trying to communicate. This wildly popular book explains how differences can come between the sexes and prohibit mutually fulfilling loving relationships.

How to Talk So Your Mate Will Listen and Listen So Your Mate Will Talk by Nancy L. Van Pelt (Revell, 1989).

This book presents a variety of techniques and strategies for developing skills to establish and sustain healthy communication. Among the topics are listening through nonverbals, creative questioning, marital bonding, and his-and-her talk styles. Each chapter is integrated with spiritual understanding and biblical principles.

Communication: Key to Your Marriage by H. Norman Wright (Regal, 1974).

A classic in many ways, this book has taught many couples over the years the fundamentals to good communication. It contains ten practical principles for building your partner's self-esteem, ten methods for handling angry feelings, ten steps to avoiding worry, and so on. This book is chock-full of guidelines you can use to enrich and deepen your communication.

CHAPTER TWO:

QUESTIONS ABOUT CONFLICT

When we were dating we had a fight every now and then, but that pales in comparison to what it's been like since we've been married. I know some couples who say they never fight, and that makes me all the more nervous about my marriage. Does having conflicts mean that we will get a divorce?

Like you, we have heard some mature couples, married for decades, who say that in all their years of marriage they have never had one single fight. Pretty impressive, huh? But in all honesty, we often wonder about these couples. They seem so proud, like not having conflict is the goal of marriage. Actually, it makes us wonder how deep their conversations get if they never lead to conflict. These couples must surely walk on eggshells from time to time.

You see, the goal of marriage is not to avoid conflict. Conflict—if handled correctly—can help build a stronger marriage. We have said it at least a hundred times: *Conflict is the price smart couples pay for a deepening sense of intimacy.* Without conflict it is difficult to peel away the superficial layers of a relationship and discover who we really are. When Ruth Graham was asked if she and her famous husband Billy ever fight, she said, "I hope so. Otherwise we would have no differences, and life would be pretty boring."

Consider the reasons for marital spats. First of all, people are not perfect, and neither is the world we live in. And while it makes logical sense that there are no perfect marriages, many of us still expect *our* marriage to be different. This expectation alone is enough to set off countless conflicts. Another factor that adds fuel to the fire of marital fights is the human tendency to resist compromise. Every day couples run up against desires, big and small, that collide with each other. For example, a husband wants to work overtime to acquire enough money to make a down payment on a house, while the wife would rather sacrifice the savings and spend more time together at home. There is no real right or wrong side in this scenario. Both partners have a good point. But a compromise is needed if they are ever going to resolve it. Yet for most people, compromise is difficult, and conflict is thus inevitable.

We could go on listing reasons for turbulence in marriage. But no matter how deeply a man and woman love each other, they *will* encounter conflict. It is a natural component of every healthy marriage. So don't bury your differences. Instead, view them as a potential source for cultivating a deeper sense of intimacy. Of course, to do this, you must learn to fight fair. And this is covered in the next question.

I've never thought of arguing as being good for a marriage. What exactly do you mean by this, and how can we learn to fight fair?

Some time ago a couple came to see us because they were scared to death of getting a divorce. They had been married a couple of years and both had come from homes where their parents had split. Every time this young couple encountered a potential conflict, they buried it. If they got into an argument, they reasoned, divorce was only a few steps away. As a result, they were both walking around like a couple of simmering volcanoes wondering which one was going to erupt first.

This couple, like so many others we have seen, mistakenly assumed that if their marriage was free from conflict, if they could just repress it and stomp it out, they could protect their union from divorce. This belief is a myth. The truth is that buried conflict has a high rate of resurrection. If something is bothering one of you, it is always best to put it out on the table and discuss it. The bottom line is this: Far more important than *whether* you argue is *how* you argue. So here are a few tips on how to fight fair.

First, when you are experiencing tension in your relationship, plan a peace conference. Don't ignore the conflict, hoping it will disappear. Set a mutually agreeable "appointment" time to discuss what is bothering you. This takes initiative, but it is critically important to schedule a face-to-face meeting if you are to resolve conflict in your relationship.

Next, cultivate a win-win attitude. In other words, seek to understand your partner's perspective before trying to "prove your case." Too many spouses become instant attorneys when it comes to marital conflict, convincing an invisible jury that they have been treated unjustly and that their partner should be found guilty. Don't fall for this fallacy. Instead, put yourself in your partner's shoes and try to see the world from his or her perspective. In fighting fair, the point is not to prove your partner wrong and win; the goal is to understand one another so you both win.

This leads to another tip: Attack the problem, not the person. You are not going to change your spouse through arguing. Our natural impulse during conflict is to defend and protect our position, not to accommodate the other person, even when it's our spouse. If you accuse your spouse of always making you late, she is probably not going to say, "Oh, you're right. I'll be different from now on." She is more likely to tell you that you only make it worse by pressuring her, or that you are too impatient, or a hundred other reasons why she is not at fault. You will be far more productive if you focus on the problem of being late and work together, as a team, to devise a way of avoiding it. In other words, separate the problem from your partner.

To sum up the idea of fighting fair, you must be cooperative. You must be willing to flex and yield to your partner. Scripture says, "Wisdom . . . is peace-loving and courteous. It allows discussion and is willing to yield to others; it is full of mercy and good deeds. It is wholehearted and straightforward and sincere" (James 3:17 TLB). If you decide to have a cooperative attitude with your partner, you will save yourself and your marriage a lot of unnecessary grief. And you will have found the secret to fighting fair.

Whenever a conflict erupts between us, it eventually ends with one of us checking out, either emotionally or physically leaving the room. This has become a fairly predictable pattern, and it seems to get us nowhere. What are we doing wrong?

Few things are more destructive to your marriage than coping with conflict by withdrawing. And since this has become a repetitive way of dealing with your conflict, it is particularly important that you take note of some important research conducted by Dr. John Gottman of the University of Washington. For more than twenty years, he has been studying marriages and has identified the signs in conflict that almost always spell disaster.[1] He calls them "The Four Horsemen of the Apocalypse." And when they gallop into your relationship, danger is imminent.

We first talked about these horsemen in *Saving Your Marriage Before It Starts*, but they are so critically important to fighting fair that they deserve to be repeated here. The first is *criticism*. This is different from complaining, which generally focuses on behavior. Criticism focuses on the person: "You never turn off the hall light." Complaining, on the other hand, would say: "I feel frustrated when the hall light is left on." It may seem like a subtle difference, but research shows that this fine line makes a significant difference in your quarrel quotient. To keep them straight, remember this general rule: Criticism usually begins with "You . . ." and entails blaming, making a personal attack or an accusation, while complaining begins with "I . . ." and is a negative comment about something you wish were otherwise.

The next toxic sign to avoid in your fighting is *contempt.* This is name-calling, humiliation, and hostile humor intended to insult and harm your partner. Contempt will poison every marriage. Once it is let loose, its venom does damage in ways we never could have imagined. Contempt comes when we say, for example, "You are such a jerk; I can't believe you have to be reminded about every little thing in this house." It can also be conveyed much more subtly with a roll of the eyes or a sarcastic glance. Contempt causes our partner to feel belittled and hurt.

Contempt often leads to the next negative sign: *defensiveness.* After all, who wouldn't put up their guard in response to a belittling spouse. "You were the one who turned the light on, not me!" These kinds of defensive statements become a reflex in homes where contempt is used. As understandable as this response is, however, it is still destructive. Why? Because the conflict escalates in the face of defenses rather than getting resolved.

The final "horseman" is *stonewalling,* which occurs when couples reach rock bottom. Feeling overwhelmed by emotions, stonewallers withdraw by presenting a "stone wall" response. They try to keep their faces immobile, avoid eye contact, hold their necks rigid, and avoid nodding their heads or making the small sounds that would indicate they are listening. When stonewalling enters a conflict, so does icy distance and disapproval.

From your own description, you and your partner often encounter this fourth horseman. If this is true, we recommend that you waste no time in seeing a competent marriage counselor who can work with you to break this destructive pattern. The more entrenched this pattern becomes, the more difficult it is to break it. The good news is that you can learn to fight constructively no matter what your condition if you are both willing to work at it. Your conflicts don't have to lead to withdrawal. So get the help your marriage needs. It just might be the most important thing you ever do for each other.

My husband and I try to practice the principles of fighting fair and do pretty well most of the time. However, on some issues we simply do not see eye to eye. What should we do when we can't agree?

No two people agree on everything. You may be quite skilled at communicating as a couple, and you may be fairly agreeable in demeanor, but there still may be times when you simply can't agree. Whether it be over what color to paint the kitchen or how many children to have, you will eventually find areas where you can't seem to find a satisfactory solution.

When you run up against such a disagreement, however, don't despair. Some things can help you manage the disagreement, if not resolve it. To begin with, decide whether this disagreement is worth fighting for. Little things, such as disagreeing on whether the movie you just saw had a plausible plot, are the stuff of interesting conversation and can be enjoyed as simple differences of opinion. And even some large disagreements, such as which presidential candidate you support, are better left at a standstill where you "agree to disagree." But if you are having difficulty agreeing on more important decisions, like whose home to go to for the holidays or how much money should be spent on a new couch, you may want to try a couple of proven exercises.

The first exercise uses Conflict Cards, which are designed to help both of you stand on equal emotional ground during a disagreement. Generally, one partner is more expressive than the other on a particular topic, and Conflict Cards will insure that each person is being accurately understood. The cards contain a scale from one to ten ranking the intensity of a person's feelings:

1. "I'm not enthusiastic, but it's no big deal to me."
2. "I don't see it the way you do, but I may be wrong."
3. "I don't agree, but I can live with it."
4. "I don't agree, but I'll let you have your way."
5. "I don't agree and cannot remain silent on this."
6. "I do not approve, and I need more time."
7. "I strongly disapprove and cannot go along with it."
8. "I will be so seriously upset, I can't predict my reaction."
9. "No possible way! If you do, I quit!"
10. "Over my dead body!"

Anytime you are head-to-head in a heated disagreement, you can measure the intensity of your feelings and compare notes ("This is a three for me." "It's a five for me."). By rating your conflict in this way, you can play on a level field even when one person is more expressive than the other.

If you would like a free set of Conflict Cards, please write: Conflict Card, Zondervan Direct Source, 5300 Patterson Ave. SE, Grand Rapids, MI 49530. Or you may call 1–800–727–3480.

Once you accurately understand where each of you is coming from on a particular issue, your next task is to find a compromise. If one person feels much more strongly about it, that may tip the scales in his direction, but in the fine art of compromising one person cannot *always* "win" the disagreement. Compromise means balancing the scales: If we go to your home for the holidays this year, we will go to mine the next. When two mature people can bend and flex in this way, they may not agree on everything, but they keep their marriage strong. As a Scottish proverb says, "Better bend than break."

One more thing about reaching a compromise. Once the two of you have made your decision, move on. Don't try to win sympathy or second-guess your partner. You've made a joint decision to compromise, and that settles it. Focus on positive things. It will make your next disagreement that much easier.

A few days ago, my wife and I had this blowout fight just before we were headed out the door for a bite to eat. The silly thing is that I can't even remember what the issue was. It sure seemed important at the time, but it obviously wasn't a major issue. Why do we argue over little things?

Isn't it ridiculous? You find yourself bickering over the smallest of matters: when to go through a traffic signal, how to make spaghetti, the way toothpaste should be squeezed, which video to rent, how the bathroom sink got so dirty, and on and on.

One of the biggest reasons for arguing over little things comes down to offering unsolicited advice. You know you do it; we all do. We can't seem to stop ourselves from pointing out little areas where our spouse needs to do, say, think, or feel something different. But it is amazing how much needless confrontation in a marriage can be avoided when we simply bite our tongues and keep from spouting off suggestions (let alone commands).

Unsolicited advice is about as welcome as an IRS audit. It implies that your partner is incapable of doing something on his or her own, and it feels like a put-down from someone with a superior attitude. Nobody likes to have a "boss" for a spouse. Even if you offer the advice or suggestion with loving intentions, your spouse is still likely to hear it as a negative critique, and it will probably lead to conflict.

So how can you avoid fighting over little things? One of the smartest actions successful couples take is to *ask* their partner before launching into a Dear Abby mode. They say something like, "I know you didn't ask for my opinion, but would you mind if I tell you what I'm thinking?" If a partner isn't open to a suggestion like this, then it is best to keep it to yourself and save yourself an unnecessary argument. On the other hand, your partner may welcome your input, and you can give it a helpful tone.

Before you offer free advice to your partner, pause and ask for permission. You will save yourself from a needless argument over something stupid.

I love my spouse more than words can describe, but he holds the potential to hurt me more deeply than anyone on earth. With a harsh comment or mean word he can inflict a bruise on my spirit that takes weeks to heal. Do I need to forgive my husband for things he says or does?

I (Leslie) asked this same question not long into our new marriage. Les had made a critical comment about the way I organized a cabinet in our kitchen. I can't even recall what he said, but at the time, it hurt me. I know now that as a new wife I was eager to please and thus easily offended. I also know now that Les did not intend to cause me pain, but nonetheless, he did. And seeking to be a good person, I quietly forgave him for his "critical attitude" and "painful words."

It took me some time, but I eventually realized that I was frequently forgiving Les for hurtful words or actions he didn't even know he had made. A wise counselor helped me see that my forgiveness was, in reality, preventing me from confronting the issues that irritated me and thus I was missing out on an opportunity to better understand my husband and learn how to improve the way we interacted. My trigger-happy forgiveness was blocking the real work of facing up to conflicts, a prospect I desperately wanted to avoid.

On the other hand, I have also learned that not every remark or action is innocent and that our marriage could never survive without moments of sincere forgiveness. When deep pain has been caused, forgiveness is the only path to healing. Any marriage that goes the distance, in fact, is made up not of two good lovers, but of two good forgivers. Forgiveness is a prerequisite to fulfillment in marriage. No matter how loving you are, you are bound to hurt your spouse and be hurt in return. And there is no way to have genuine love in your marriage if one or both of you are seething inside because of some hurtful words or actions.

Forgiveness is God's prescription for helping couples heal inevitable marital wounds. "Bear with each other and forgive whatever grievances you may have against one another," writes Paul in Colossians 3:13. "Forgive as the Lord forgave you."

Years of heartache can be prevented if you learn to forgive your partner early on. Time and again, we have seen deep-rooted problems in marriage traced back to years of being unwilling to forgive a partner for their misdeeds. Sometimes the offense is quite minor, but it gradually grows until it produces overwhelming bitterness. And it could have all been avoided had the couple practiced forgiveness early on in their marriage.

So what sorts of things require forgiveness in marriage? Burnt toast? Lost sunglasses? Forgetting a birthday? Maybe. And maybe not. Forgiveness is not something that should be tossed around here and there like salt from a saltshaker. Forgiveness is a solemn and intentional act of grace that is given when we have been deeply hurt. It is needed to heal the pain of being wronged by the person we trusted.

To be a good forgiver, therefore, you must be in touch with your feelings. You must know what pain feels like. While it is sometimes tempting to deny the pain your partner causes, it will only come back to brutalize your marriage. Repressed pain has a high rate of resurrection. So to begin the process of forgiveness, you must *accept* the unfair hurt.

Next, we must realize that every painful feeling does not require forgiveness. When your partner drives you crazy by switching channels mindlessly on the television set, for example, you may feel annoyed, but you are not seriously hurt. To offer forgiveness for such an annoyance would only cheapen it. Forgiveness is not for feelings of annoyance. Nor is it for feelings of disappointment. Your spouse may not think to buy your favorite cereal on a trip to the grocery, but disappointment is not the same as betrayal, and you don't need to forgive disappointments.

Forgiveness is reserved for deep feelings of hurt. When you feel that your partner has intentionally wounded you or been unfair, it is time for forgiveness. In fact, *the best indicator we know of for determining when it is time to forgive is when you feel like getting even.* Forgiveness releases us from the pain of the past by surrendering our desire to make our spouse suffer too.

Forgiveness prevents destructive attitudes from getting a toehold in your marriage. If you do not offer forgiveness to your spouse, your life and your marriage will become full of bitterness and anger. The nineteenth-century Scottish author and preacher George MacDonald said that unwillingness to forgive is a greater sin than murder. With murder, the deed is done and complete; unforgiveness destroys for a lifetime.

When my wife disagrees with me, she often gives me the silent treatment. She won't want to talk about the issue until she is ready, and sometimes that can be days later. What should I do?

Some people deal with potential conflict by simply avoiding issues about which they might disagree. They might postpone discussion about a problem to a later time, or they might simply ignore it altogether. Some couples deny that a problem exists at all. Still other couples are prone to withdraw from conflict by shutting down or actually leaving.

Does avoiding conflict affect marriage? You bet. But the effect depends on the answers to two crucial questions: Who chooses the tactic? and How long is the problem avoided?

Husband and wife can choose the avoidance tactic jointly as a way of dealing with conflict, or, as in your case, avoidance can be chosen by one partner and then imposed on the other. Some married couples jointly agree to handle conflict by avoiding it because each feels very uncomfortable fighting with the other. And these jointly agreed-upon avoidance tactics can work okay for some marriages. But when only one partner chooses avoidance and imposes it on the other, the marriage is more threatened. Such one-sided avoidance might actually become another source of conflict.

The question of how long avoidance goes on is also critical to the long-term prospects for the marriage. Temporarily avoiding problems, providing they are addressed later, does not necessarily have a negative impact on the marriage. However, indefinitely avoided and thus unsolved marital conflicts can ultimately lead to further problems. The bottom line is that avoiding disagreements may work okay for the relationship in the short run, but in the long run, it often leads to the relationship's deterioration.

So here is our suggestion. Keep track of conflict avoidance in your relationship for a couple months so you know, objectively, how frequently and on what issues your spouse seems to avoid talking about tough issues. Also track how long it takes her to come around to a previously avoided discussion. With this data you are much better equipped to intervene if necessary. However, you may find that her avoidance is not nearly so frequent as you imagined.

If her avoidance occurs several times within two or three months and if she seldom comes back to being willing to discuss hot topics, we recommend that both of you seek the objective help of a reputable marriage counselor. A professional can intervene to help you avoid getting too entrenched in a dangerous pattern and begin to deal with tough issues in a more open and healthy manner.

If my wife wants to avoid conflict indefinitely, I have a hard time believing that this could have long-term implications for the well-being of our marriage. Is it really that serious of a problem?

Allow us to say it plainly: The permanent avoidance of conflict-inducing problems by an unsatisfied partner not only reduces marital satisfaction but also may endanger the survival of the marriage itself. We don't say this to frighten you, but only to underscore the seriousness of the problem.

Diane Vaughan, author of *Uncoupling*, describes what happens when couples fail to communicate their dissatisfaction.[2] In her study, couples began to "uncouple" when one partner became dissatisfied with the relationship but refused to discuss the dissatisfaction openly with the partner. Instead, the unhappy spouse tried to "fix" the relationship (for example, by trying to get the partner to change in some way) without talking to the partner about the problem. When attempts to fix the relationship in this way failed, the dissatisfied partner became convinced that the relationship could not be salvaged and began to look for a way to end the relationship.

Vaughan's work suggests that the lack of open discussion about problems dooms many relationships. In the uncouplings she studied, the dissatisfied partner had given up on the relationship before the other partner was aware there was a serious problem. By the time the other partner discovered there was a problem, the dissatisfied partner already wanted out.

Not being willing to voice one's frustrations to a spouse can be like a toxin to a marriage. If the avoidance is not corrected, it is a definite sign of danger.

What are some of the most helpful resources on conflict in marriage?

Why Marriages Succeed or Fail by John Gottman (Simon & Schuster, 1994).

Based on a twenty-year study of more than 2,000 married couples, this book pinpoints just what makes marriage work. According to the author, the most serious threats to a lasting marriage are found in how a couple handles conflict. With lucid examples and self-tests, this book will help you spot potential problem patterns in your own marriage and guide you to healthier ways of interacting.

We Can Work It Out: Making Sense of Marital Conflict by Clifford Notarious and Howard Markman (Putnam, 1993).

According to these authors, the key to a happy and successful marriage is a couple's ability to handle their differences. Based on groundbreaking research, the book offers an innovative three-part communication program designed to defuse any argument. With questionnaires, exercises, and anecdotes, *We Can Work It Out* is a refreshingly optimistic guidebook to resolving conflict.

Fighting for Your Marriage: Positive Steps for Preventing Divorce and Preserving a Lasting Love by Howard Markman, Scott Stanley, and Susan L. Blumberg (Jossey-Bass, 1994).

These authors bring a dauntless optimism to making marriage work. Their book is based on the highly praised PREP (Prevention and Relationship Enhancement Program) workshop and demonstrates the kinds of techniques that have proven effective for preventing marital problems. They show how men and women differ in the way they fight and seek intimacy in marriage, why adding structure to conversation can help keep hot topics from turning into marital meltdowns, and so on.

CHAPTER THREE:
QUESTIONS ABOUT CAREERS

I work part-time to help with the bills, but I'm mostly a tradi-tional stay-at-home wife, and I like it that way. However, my hus-band, who is just beginning his career, seems to think his work shouldn't concern me, and as a result I feel left out. I'm not a control monger, but I'd like to be included in his career plans. Do you think that's wrong?

"What do you want to be when you grow up?" is a chal-lenging question to answer when you are three years old. At age eighteen, or sometimes earlier, there comes another one: "Have you decided what you are going to do with your life?" Then comes the inquiry heard over and over before retirement: "What do you do for a living?" It sometimes seems our society is obsessed with occupations and careers. In turn, our identity is linked to our career choice. And, in a very real sense, so is our marriage.

The decisions you or your husband will be making during your work life hold the potential to influence your marriage dra-matically. Career decisions are not isolated in a compartment totally separate from your home life. Your husband may leave work at the office, but work won't leave him (remember, it's part of our identity). Since work plays such a dominant role in our lives, it cannot help but impact our marriage. That's why charting a career path together is critically important to the health of your marriage.

Just as you couldn't plan a trip without knowing the desired destination, you and your spouse are unwise to map out a career track unless you know your objective. This decision doesn't have to be made immediately, but chances are that you and your spouse are already on a trajectory that is taking you someplace. The question remains, however, is it the place that you and your partner want to go together?

Talking about where each of you will be ten, twenty, thirty years from now can help you gain control and chart the course each of you feels good about. Many overlook the need to integrate career with marriage, but since work holds the potential to interfere with marriage on the negative side or augment one's married life on the positive side, we feel strongly that it is time well spent.

So we encourage you to set aside some serious time to establish career goals together. Consider everything from relocation possibilities, business travel, promotions, income, and flexibility. Ask yourselves how each aspect could impact your marriage. Also, consider the kinds of work-related issues that you would expect to have influence on together. The more you talk about these matters, the closer you will come to building a career path that is in sync with your marriage.

We both work and have a very full calendar. With worthwhile commitments to our jobs, as well as to our church, we are often beat when we have time at home. It seems like we rarely have quality time with each other. How do we keep our busy schedules under control?

We're in the same boat and can completely identify with your question. Each of us has worked full-time (if you count graduate school) our entire married life. And like you, we have always been active in our church, often teaching classes and working with the youth group. For many years, it seemed that we rarely had time alone where we were not exhausted. It took us a while, and we still continue to battle our busy schedules, but we've learned some important lessons in finding quality time together.

Time is a valuable commodity when both partners work. After an exhausting day, each person comes home to negotiate dinner. Dirty dishes require attention, someone needs to pay the bills, the lawn needs mowing, shopping must be done, and there is an endless stream of laundry to be washed. Oh, and then there is a social life. Oh, and a love life . . . if you are lucky.

The increased pressure on home time due to long hours at work and inflexible work schedules means that much less of a couple's time can be devoted to recreation, play, self-renewal, and each other. When both husband and wife work, they will not necessarily have less time together, but the time they have together will be consumed by daily necessities.

So what can be done to rescue quick-fading hours?

Believe it or not, one of the biggest reasons dual-worker families have difficulty finding time to spend on their marriages is that the husbands, research has shown us, do not shoulder their fair share of household tasks.[1] Returning home from a long day's work to do more work is hardly an inviting prospect. But for a variety of reasons housework is, more often than not, left to the wife. If you want to find a few more hours to devote to each other, evaluate who is doing what when you are home. Make a list of household chores, how long they take to do, and who does them. If you discover an imbalance in household assignments, make some changes and redistribute the housework more evenly.

Another common theft of valuable couple-time is found in extending the workday. Do you bring work home, either concretely or psychologically? The dawn of computers, fax machines, and cellular phones has made it possible to work anywhere, anytime. This can be beneficial at times and harmful at other times.

A career-oriented spouse is much more apt to bring work home than is a family-oriented partner. So check it out. Is your spouse resenting the time you spend at your computer? Are you "married to your job" instead of your partner? If so, set some limits. Determine when you will work at home if you need to, and schedule it with your partner's time in mind.

If you can make it a habit to "check in" with each other after each workday to get a read on one another's day and current emotional tone, you will be doing a tremendous thing for your marriage. This simple ritual can save you hours of wondering why your partner is so stressed or why they don't seem present with you. Listen to your partner's feelings and do what you can to help ease their load when they are home. If he or she needs some downtime alone, make it happen. If they need some levity, make them laugh. The point is to put yourself in their shoes and make life a little easier.

Don't allow your dual-career marriage to become a two-person-separate-lives marriage.

I'm a working woman. I went to college to be a graphic designer and landed a great job shortly after graduation. In fact, I earn more than my husband. However, my parents are convinced that since I work outside the home, our marriage is going to fall apart. Is there any evidence to show that a wife's working leads to marriage problems?

The relationship of work and family in the United States has undergone a profound change in the last few decades. More and more women have entered the labor force. In the past, most women in the workplace were single. Now married women, often with children under eighteen, are entering the labor force in unprecedented numbers. This has created the "dual-worker" family, and only recently have researchers been able to uncover its effect on marriage.

There is little doubt that the working woman's ability to support herself financially has led to a stronger sense of independence. In the past a woman's reliance on her husband for financial support contributed to her staying in the marriage bond. Now a woman alone can survive financially. But not only did a woman in the past have fewer economic alternatives than her husband, she also had to derive her status from his success. Not so for today's working woman. She can carve out her own professional identity separate from his. Of course this new independence (financially and professionally) can be viewed as contributing to the breakup of some marriages.

On the other side of the coin, studies have shown that work outside the home can improve and enhance a woman's family life. Her earnings can increase the family's standard of living and alleviate the family's monetary restraints. In addition, the working wife may derive great personal satisfaction from her work and this, in turn, can stimulate a more fulfilling marriage. Her self-esteem may increase with the knowledge that she is a more equal partner in the marriage.[2]

As you can see, research evidence on marital satisfaction when the wife works is mixed. After reviewing many studies, researchers have concluded that wives who work from choice rather than economic necessity, those whose husbands view their employment favorably, and those who work part-time are happier with their marriages than full-time housewives.[3] Whether a wife works cannot be consistently related to marital satisfaction. *How* couples cope with the wife working, not whether the wife works, is the most important determiner of a positive or a negative impact on the marriage.

For many couples a dual-career family is inevitable, and these couples must intentionally focus on balancing their careers with their marriage—so their jobs work for them and not the other way around. Once a couple works out the new routines and relationship changes, marital satisfaction need not suffer and, with the right attitudes, can be strengthened all the more.

We are both career minded. Before we even got married, we decided to respect one another's professional pursuits and support each other as a team. We are now realizing that our career pursuits can sometimes clash. So we are wondering—whose career should take priority?

In the age of the dual-income couple, relocation may mean dragging a spouse out of a job. It seems that one person's career will eventually call the couple to determine whose work takes priority. Granted, for many traditional couples that question is already settled. A couple, for example, with traditional gender-role values will see the husband as primary provider and decision maker. But if you are asking the question of career priority, you are like the growing number of couples who are pursuing individual careers and struggling to find an answer to this quandary.

Of the twenty-two million people who packed up and moved for work in 1993, only two million were husbands going along with their wives.[4] While that's double the number from 1980, it's a sluggish progression, considering the large number of women who have reached middle- and upper-management, positions ripe for relocation assignments. Still, the dilemma of whose career should take priority is popular enough now to have a name. "The Trailing Spouse Crisis" hit the front page of the *Wall Street Journal* and the *New York Times* not long ago. One husband interviewed in these articles complained that after three moves to follow his wife, "I have never been able to remain in one position long enough to find out how successful I might have been in my own career."

The issue comes down to what you, as a couple, value most. Once you determine what matters most to both of you, your decisions on how to allocate time and priorities fall more easily into place. So permit us to ask: Would your decision to move for work simply be a matter of maximizing your financial well-being? A study by the Mobil Corporation found that a man generally will follow his wife only if she earns at least forty percent more than he does. Is that true of you? What about prestige and power? Is your professional priority in climbing the ladder? If so, does that mean that if your spouse is moving up faster than you, then his or her job takes precedence over yours?

Typically the priority gap can't be explained and settled by salary and stature alone. There is much more that goes into determining the actual balance of power in your relationship. In fact, you might find that one person's career takes precedence over the other's for a period of time and then, years into the marriage, the order of priority is exchanged.

Determining whose career should take priority is a matter of each couple's personal journey. Sociologist Arlie Hochschild, author of *The Second Shift*, found that many people ideologically support the idea of egalitarian roles, in carrying out those roles in valuing each other's careers, the principles get lost. What people say they believe about marital roles often contradicts what they seem to *feel* about them.[5]

So to prioritize your respective careers you will need to do some soul-searching. You will need to be honest with each other and communicate your real feelings. Once you begin the process of openly discussing your desires for your careers, you will eventually come closer to balancing the power and respecting one another's goals. Remember, however, that it is a process for most couples.

The quick solution on this issue is rare, as we found in our own experience. Early on in our marriage it became evident that both of us valued higher education and wanted to pursue advanced degrees. However, each of us set our sights on earning doctorates, not so much because we had individual career paths in mind, but because we wanted to stay on equal footing in our relationship. We had seen several examples of one-up-one-down relationships and decided that wasn't for us. With school bills, however, we had to take turns getting our degrees. We had a general plan, not a tidy step-by-step design, that brought us to where we are. And it took our first decade of marriage to achieve our shared dream of two doctorates. Like we said, prioritizing respective careers in marriage does not happen overnight.

My husband eats, drinks, and breathes work. It's not that he is always satisfied with his job, but he is constantly thinking and talking about it, even on vacations. I'm glad he is dedicated to his job, but sometimes, when I am honest, I feel a little jealous of his work. I know I am more important to him than his career, but it doesn't always feel that way. Why is he so consumed by it?

More time and energy are spent in work than in any other waking activity. Sixty-eight percent of us spend more than nine hours each day on the job, including getting to and from work. And more than one in five of all employed adults bring work home at least twice a week.

Work is consuming. We complain about work. We try to avoid work. We call in sick to get out of work. But the truth is that we need purposeful work—not for the money alone, but for a sense of personal worth.

Work provides more than financial rewards. It provides spiritual, psychological, and emotional support as well. Sigmund Freud said that to live well we must learn to love well *and* to work well. Kahlil Gibran said, "Work is love made visible."

For most of us, work, whether paid or unpaid, gives us our identity. Work brings personal fulfillment. Leigh Hunt said, "Occupation is the necessary basis of all enjoyment." Thomas

Carlyle said, "Work is the grand cure of all the maladies and miseries that ever plagued humankind."

We love to hate work while we hate to admit we love it. Cartoonists and storytellers have assumed that most people who toil for their daily bread fantasize about winning the lottery, telling the boss what he can do with his old job, kicking the Xerox machine, packing up their Rolodex, and hitting the road. But this is a false picture. In a national survey, more than three-fourths of the respondents said they would choose to remain in their same jobs even though they had, by good fortune, received enough money to live comfortably for the rest of their lives.

Perhaps you are thinking people *need* to say that to feel good about their jobs. Maybe you are wondering what they would really do if it actually happened. The Institute for Socio-Economic Studies wondered the same thing. They looked up more than 1,000 people who had won a million dollars or more in a lottery. Only sixteen percent actually retired from work altogether. And four out of ten kept working at the same job they had even though they had no need for the income.

What then draws people like your husband so strongly to work? An important part of the answer is found in relationships. Marsha Sinetar, author of *Do What You Love and the Money Will Follow*, writes, "Through work and relationships the individual finds a place in the world, belongs to it, and takes responsibility for himself and for others. Work becomes his way of giving of himself. His work or vocation provides him with a way of dedicating himself to live. Through it, he cultivates his talents, stands in for others, exhibits his involvement and connection to the world."

All this is to say that the time and energy one spends on work is not necessarily unhealthy—as long as it is balanced with spiritual and family priorities that come through just as strongly. Without knowing more about your husband and your relationship, however, it is difficult for us to say whether this is the case for your husband. Your questioning of the amount of time and energy he puts into work, however, is a red flag to us that he may, indeed, be out of balance, so let's see if we can help.

If the two of you were to come into our office for counseling, we would explore your husband's growing-up years to discover the kinds of standards his parents set for him. Our hunch is that they were quite high. If so, this is a tip-off to some underlying feelings of inferiority and a need to prove his worth. We might find that your husband equates who he is with what he does. That's a deadly trip, but even more potentially lethal is how he views work itself. For most people, work is a means to an end, but if he is out of balance he probably views work as an end in itself. If this is the case we offer several specific suggestions.

First, we would encourage him to recognize the lie of believing that he is what he does. We would encourage him to rest in the fact that he is a child of God and does not have to scurry around proving he is worthy. "Come to me, all you who are weary and burdened, and I will give you rest. For my yoke is easy and my burden is light" (Matthew 11:28–30). Next, we would encourage both of you, as a team, to get serious about having fun. When a person is out of balance at work, he or she has usually forgotten how to play. Most importantly, however, we would challenge your husband to clarify his priorities by writing them down and then asking him to describe the evidence for placing them where he does. This is usually the clincher for someone whose work has taken control of his or her life. It generally sounds the alarm for action and helps them to realize that they need to do something radical to live out their priorities.

Transforming a workaholic is not usually an instantaneous experience. So don't be too tough on your husband, but don't be afraid to keep him accountable to the things that matter most.

Okay, so I understand how important my husband's career is to him, but he has become so stressed out about it that I think he is going to burn out. He is working harder than ever, and I am afraid he is going to have a heart attack or something. What kind of advice would you give my husband to keep work in perspective and manage his stress?

Work stress is usually a response to constant emotional strain and it leads to a sense of personal ineffectiveness and eventual exhaustion. Cynicism replaces idealism, and burnout kicks in. Here are a half dozen of the most effective ways of combating burnout and managing work-related stress:

1. *Adjust expectations and set realistic goals.* This does not mean giving up ideals and becoming apathetic. It does mean setting achievable goals based on an honest appraisal of one's abilities and values.

2. *Do your job differently; vary your work routines.* Determine which parts of the job can be changed and which cannot. Analyze the consequences of a change in work procedures. Talking to coworkers or your supervisor or taking a workshop or seminar may give you some new ideas about doing your job. Taking action may not be easy, but constant frustration is worse.

3. *Get away from the job for a while.* Getting away can involve a time period ranging from a fifteen-minute coffee break to a one-hour lunch period to a day, a week, or a month. Use a sick day or a vacation period if necessary. Avoid working through lunch hours or coming back to the office in the evening to catch up on work.

4. *Get enough rest and relaxation.* Get sufficient sleep. Use relaxation techniques such as muscle relaxation and deep-breathing exercises. Change pace and wind down after work. Listen to music. Meditate. Engage in a vigorous physical activity. Become absorbed in a hobby. Do something to leave the strains of the job behind.

5. *Seek satisfactions outside of work.* Open up your life beyond the boundaries of your work environment. Family and friends can offer encouragement when work problems thicken. Outside activities and relationships provide outlets for creativity and challenge.

6. *Keep the Sabbath day holy.* From the beginning God blessed and hallowed a Sabbath day. God the Creator himself, after six days of activity, sanctified a seventh day of rest. The Sabbath is a divine institution for rest, relaxation, and worship. "There remains, then, a Sabbath-rest for the people of God; for anyone who enters God's rest also rests from his own work, just as God did from his" (Hebrews 4:9).

Good jobs are steeped in annoyances, pressures, and problems. The truth is, human labor is no more God's curse than life itself. Though the Fall tainted work, we can't forget that God introduced the concept of human labor *before* the Fall. When Adam and Eve were still innocent of sin, God gave them jobs to do. He called Adam to name the animals, then asked Adam and Eve to subdue the animals, manage the Garden of Eden, and prepare food from the plants and trees. Why would a loving God put his children to work as soon as he created them? Because he knew human labor is a blessing. He knew that even with all its foibles, work would provide one of the greatest sources of human satisfaction. But without a strategic plan to avoid frustration, fatigue, and even disillusionment, every worker is walking dangerously close to burnout.

A friend of ours recently lost his job, and he and his wife are not holding up well. We feel terrible about their situation and we also feel afraid that something like that could happen to us. What advice do you have on surviving a career crisis?

The word *career* in Latin is translated as "progress along a difficult road." In Greek, *crisis* is the "decisive moment." Thus, a career crisis may be thought of as "a decisive moment on a long and difficult road." And if you are wise, you will not expect your career path to be smooth. It is almost inevitable that at some point you will run into a jolt or two. And being prepared as a couple for this time just may be what carries you through it successfully.

If you are thinking you won't experience a career crisis, don't count on it. Barry Glassner, in his best-selling book *Career Crash*, states, "Career crashes have become a predictable crisis in many baby boomers' lives, as defining of their middle years as Vietnam or Watergate were for their youth."[6] Glassner compares the nostalgic career journey of the past generation to a calm drive in the countryside, and underscores that this is what most boomers may have anticipated for their own futures. What they actually find is that the career journey is more like a roller-coaster ride whose contours are shaped by economic turbulence, a penchant for change, and a basic anxiety—even despair—about the demands of life.

What can you expect when you or your spouse experiences a career crisis? Regardless of the specific context, a career crisis typically creates a wide range of intense emotions, including shame, guilt, anger, self-loathing, denial, shock, and even relief. But one of the most debilitating parts of the aftermath of job loss or any other career crisis is self-blame. Although individuals in career crisis feel that they have been treated unjustly, they also believe they have been the cause of their own injustice. Journalist Harry Maurer has interviewed hundreds of people struggling with job loss and states, "Unemployed people feel they have been robbed of something, yet on a deeper level they feel it was their fault."[7]

Dr. Greiff, a consulting psychiatrist to Harvard University's Health Service in Cambridge, Massachusetts, likens job loss to the humiliation that lurks in the proverbial nightmare about being found naked in a public place. "In our society, you are what you do, and that gets stripped from you when you get fired. You become, in a sense, vocationally naked."[8]

This being the case, a spouse can help his or her partner move through the crisis by, first of all, being supportive and affirming. Any form of criticism or complaint is terribly damaging in this stage. But another practical way a spouse can help is to give attention to helping the spouse maintain a positive structure in their daily lives. It is important for unemployed persons to continue participating in regular activities. It boosts their morale and provides the fuel they need for maintaining a growing and productive stance in the season between jobs.

One of the most positive impacts of a career crisis is the window of opportunity it creates for career change. Losing a job may give the license needed to consider opportunities that have only been dreamed about in the past. And a supportive spouse can make a tremendous difference in the process. Encouraging words or even a positive presence can help a hurting spouse transcend self-blame and move on. There is no way to escape the pain of a career crisis or job loss, but with a committed spouse, survival and recovery is much easier.

What are some of the most helpful resources on careers and marriage?

How to Work with the One You Love and Live to Tell About It by Cameron and Donna Partow (Bethany House, 1995).

If you work in the same company, volunteer on the same committees, or put up wallpaper together, this book lays out the potential problems and helps you solve them before they get serious. The Partows show you how to evaluate the pros and cons of working together, manage risk, build accountability without nagging or dominating, and resolve conflict. If you work together or plan to, this one is worth a look.

Winning at Work Without Losing at Love by Stephen Arterburn (Thomas Nelson, 1994).

> Some people sacrifice just about anything for career success. Others focus exclusively on their relationships and have a difficult time making ends meet. Arterburn believes you don't have to have one without the other—you can be a winner in both business and marriage. He shows you how to establish a solid foundation for success at work and at home. He teaches you how to set achievable goals that create a win/win situation for everyone.

Achieving Success Without Failing Your Family by Paul Faulkner (Howard, 1994).

> Some "experts" say you cannot have both career success and family excellence. This book proves them wrong. It is the story of thirty families who have practiced proven strategies for building successful careers and strong families. Through their examples you will learn the importance of family traditions, the principle of being intentional, and so on. This book is particularly relevant when children become part of your home.

The Career Counselor by Les and Leslie Parrott (Word, 1995).

> Written for people who are serious about charting their lifelong career path and staying afloat in today's rapidly changing job market, this book notes four mistakes to avoid in any career decision, surefire ways to assess and market your own job skills, seven keys to bouncing back from a crushing job loss, and practical ways to snap the paralysis of indecision.

Chapter Four:

Questions About Emotions

My wife doesn't always have a lot of self-confidence. She hardly ever speaks out in public, has a terrible fear of being embarrassed, and sometimes views innocent acts as personal attacks. How can I increase my mate's self-esteem?

When we don't value ourselves and our abilities, we are likely to be extremely sensitive and edgy. It's a fact. Our attitude toward ourselves—our self-image or self-esteem—is one of the most important things we possess. It is the source of personal happiness or the lack of it. If we think little of ourselves, we either accomplish little or drive ourselves unmercifully to disprove our negative self-evaluation. Research shows that people with a positive self-concept are more at peace with themselves and those around them—including their marriage partner.[1]

When we are suffering from low self-esteem, we tend to interpret the slightest suggestion from our mate as harsh criticism. Whenever a difference of opinion crops up, we struggle to prove our point and defend our position in order to protect our shaky self-esteem. It doesn't take a clinical psychologist to see how this works. But before you go diagnosing your mate's feelings of inferiority, be aware of the fact that only one in ten Americans believes he personally suffers from low self-esteem, according to a *Newsweek* Gallup Poll, and more than fifty percent diagnose the condition in someone else in their families.[2] It seems we are trigger-happy when it comes to viewing our partner's problems as low self-esteem.

However, whether you are accurate in your diagnosis or not, improving your mate's self-esteem is an "intervention" that can never do harm. In social situations it's all too easy to tell loving couples from warring ones, based on how they treat each other. Most everyone has been at a party where one half of a couple has taken a public jab at the other. Perhaps it was along the lines of: "I keep wishing that Ron would get his duff off the couch and exercise more than his remote-control hand!" It's a bad idea to use the cover of an audience to say something you wouldn't say in private. Experts agree that couples who can't contain their criticisms in public are in serious trouble. And it is lethal to your mate's self-esteem.

Healthy couples, on the other hand, use every opportunity to boost one another in front of other people and to cast each other in the best light—much as they did in their dating days when they wanted their friends and family to like their new love. They say things like, "Ron just got a promotion, but he won't tell you that." These couples increase each other's self-esteem by being good publicists.

In their best-selling book *Building Your Mate's Self-Esteem*, Dennis and Barbara Rainey offer ten building blocks for people who want to develop their partner's self-esteem.[3] Here is a very abbreviated summary:

1. *Accept your mate unconditionally.* This is the bedrock that helps people move out of the quicksand of negative emotions.

2. *Put the past in perspective.* Understanding your partner's personal history will give both of you perspective from which to see a hopeful future.

3. *Plant positive words in your mate.* Showing appreciation of your mate's fine qualities chips away at negative self-evaluation. Affirming words reveal the image of Christ in your spouse.

4. *Encourage your mate during difficult times.* It is important to go through suffering together. When you express your need for another person, that person feels valued and worthwhile.

5. *Give your mate freedom to fail.* If your partner is terrified of failure, self-esteem is sure to be the culprit. Let him or her know that it is okay to be human. It's okay to make mistakes.

6. *Please your mate.* Let your mate know he or she is valued by doing the things that please him or her.

7. *Help your mate do what is right.* Create an environment that enhances spiritual and moral health. Model spiritual sensitivity and affirm your mate's desire to follow God.

8. *Help your mate develop friendships.* If your spouse looks only to you for encouragement, he or she may begin to wonder about other people's evaluations. Encourage friendships outside your marriage, both with couples and individuals.

9. *Help your mate keep life manageable.* When you are constantly overextended, always reacting to crises, you can't enjoy peace and contentment. Protect your spouse from hurry-sickness.

10. *Help your mate discover a sense of destiny.* Discovering a sense of purpose is one of the most important things you can do for your partner.

We are the first to admit it. Both of us are expressive people and when it comes to expressing anger, we don't hold much back. We've kind of come to accept that, but lately, it seems that anger is rearing its head a little too often. What do we do if anger is a repetitive problem?

Ron and Janet, a couple we recently counseled, had a similar problem. Like two volcanoes perpetually on the brink of eruption, they went through their first three years of marriage with an increasing sense of feeling out of control. That's what motivated them to come in and see us. We listened to their stories of angry episodes that erupted everywhere from public gatherings with strangers to holiday gatherings with their families to the confines of their own bedroom. Strangely, as they told their stories, it was apparent that they both sincerely cared for one another. Ron and Janet were deeply in love, yet volatile and quick to explode.

In the few weeks we worked with this couple, they made a lot of progress. They did not squelch their angry emotions entirely, but then that was not the goal. Allow us to summarize the information that seemed to help Ron and Janet.

First of all, marriage and anger go together. Of course any relationship can generate considerable anger, but a typical marriage relationship often generates more anger than any other.[4] Why? For one reason: The sheer amount of time spent together creates more opportunity for anger to erupt. In addition, we let our guard down with the ones we love more than we do with others. This creates opportunity not only for more intimacy but also for more frustration and anger.

But while anger comes part-and-parcel with most marriages, it should not—by a long shot—be given free license. Anger without limits can lead to terrible destruction.[5] Anger must be reined in and controlled. But how? How can a married couple cope with this inevitable feeling that holds such devastating potential? A few practical principles can help.

Successful anger management begins with recognizing, first and foremost, that anger is a natural human experience. You are not being a bad spouse just because you feel anger toward your partner. According to marriage expert David Mace, we are not responsible for being angry, only for how we respond to and use anger once it appears.[6] The apostle Paul understood this when he said, "In your anger do not sin" (Ephesians 4:26). God created us with a capacity to experience potent emotions, including the passion of anger.

With this understanding firmly in place, the next step is to recognize and admit your anger. This sounds simple, but it can be quite difficult in the heat of the fiery moment to acknowledge the feeling. Most of us want to deny the presence of anger in an attempt to control it. But that never works. Repressed anger has a high rate of resurrection. So 'fess up. Own your anger without hiding it or projecting onto your partner.

Once you have admitted your anger, the next step is to release your vindictiveness. Almost always, we become angry because we feel that someone has hurt us, and we want to hurt them back. We fool ourselves into believing that the only way to obtain satisfaction from being offended is to repay "evil for evil." Once we become consumed with balancing the score, anger takes center stage in our marriage and is destined to do damage. So practice what Jesus taught in the Sermon on the Mount: "Turn the other cheek" (Matthew 5:38–48). Paul said it this way in Romans 12:17 (TLB): "Never pay back evil for evil." This practical principle releases revenge and is an insurance policy against resentment. Practice it, and you will keep anger from ruining your marriage.

In addition to "cheek turning," here are a few more tips for keeping anger from ruling the roost:

- Be specific with your anger. What exactly is ruffling your feathers? Complete the sentence: "I'm angry because . . ."
- Return to the issue when you are calm. It is amazing what thirty minutes can do to help you collect your thoughts and diminish your anger.
- Don't allow your anger to build up until you erupt like a volcano. Deal with your hurts as they arise, one at a time.
- Listen. Once you acknowledge your anger, listen to your spouse and receive any explanation of apology that may be offered.
- Make understanding your ultimate goal. This will help you give up your angry desire to hurt back.

- If your anger has found expression in some hostile act, admit that you have crossed the line and retreat. Take time by yourself to regroup and then apologize to make it right.

If you are like most couples, anger will be a part of your marriage because you are human. But it certainly doesn't need to do its potentially damaging work. Remember, the "feeling" of anger is not harmful, it is what you do with it that matters to your marriage.

My husband suffers from depression. I love him deeply and feel terrible about his suffering, but I'm also getting tired of his ups and downs. Can you help?

For married couples, there's good news about depression: A respected study in the field of psychiatry showed that married people experience lower rates of severe depression than people who are not married.[7] The numbers were as follows (annual rate of major depression per 100):

Married (never divorced)	1.5
Never married	2.4
Divorced once	4.1
Cohabiting	5.1
Divorced twice	5.8

Wow! That's pretty significant. Married people, as a group, suffer far fewer cases of depression than other people. Before we get carried away with these statistics, however, we must still recognize that even happy couples are not immune. Depression, the "common cold of emotional problems," touches everyone's life at some point. Whether it be as a temporary mood or as a suicidal psychosis, no one is exempt—even in a loving marriage.

That's why it is critical for couples to know how to handle this emotional struggle. In fact, researchers at the University of Michigan who have studied the effect of depression on marriage found that communication deteriorates, the husband and wife avoid discussions of significant topics, conflict becomes more common, and the couple's social activities diminish. After the depression lifted, the tension often remained, and for about one-sixth of the couples the strain was so great that divorce was the result.[8]

To guard against the destructive power of depression, couples can be prepared by knowing, first of all, that some depression is normal, and is probably better thought of as feeling down or blue. However, sadness can cross the line and become debilitating if the person loses interest in normal activities, becomes easily agitated, feels inferior, helpless, or guilty. As depression worsens, the loss of energy is accompanied by sleep problems, loss of appetite or excessive eating, social withdrawal, pessimism, difficulties in concentration, and an inability to enjoy pleasurable events. The most important symptoms to watch for occur together: a sad mood and a loss of interest in one's environment.[9]

Encouraging your mate to "snap out" of these depressive symptoms rarely does any good. Often depression has a physical cause that may be as simple as a lack of rest and exercise, as common as the monthly premenstrual syndrome in some women, or as serious as biochemical malfunctioning. And even when the causes are psychological (job loss, failure, and so on), a person cannot be expected to quickly "change their attitude" and move on. Depression is a sign that a person needs time to let down and recover. In some cases, the depression will take care of itself, like a bruised knee that simply needs time to heal.

If depression persists, however, get a physical examination and professional help from a counselor. It is during this time that you must remember that your depressed mate may not be able to communicate his or her desperate need for your love and acceptance. So be patient, supportive, and understanding. A gentle hug is important during these times even if your spouse doesn't reciprocate. Ask God to bring healing to your mate's depression and to give you strength and patience during the healing process.

When one of you becomes depressed it will be very tempting for the other to become impatient, critical, frustrated, and even angry. Schedules will be disrupted, social activities will be curtailed, and joy will be sapped. But hang tight. There is hope. It may take a while, but things will get better and God will give you strength to make it—in sickness and in health.

I have a problem with guilt. It's not that I have some secret skeleton in my closet that my husband doesn't know about, I just seem to have a general disposition toward self-punishment. The littlest things—burning the toast, being late, whatever—set off my guilt alarm and I know this affects my marriage. Can you help?

In a survey assessing "who makes you feel most guilty," the majority of respondents confessed they were the key perpetrators of their own guilt. But next on the list was "my spouse." Thirty-seven percent of married people reported that their spouses control them through guilt.[10]

Guilt is that thud-in-the-gut feeling that occurs when a great gulf separates who we are and who we think we ought to be. According to Bruce Narramore, author of *No Condemnation*, this emotion is experienced in three typical forms: self-punishment, self-rejection, and self-shame.[11] Whatever form of guilt you and your partner experience, you can count on it affecting your marriage.

A fundamental distinction, however, can keep guilt from sabotaging your marriage: There is a difference between *real* guilt and *false* guilt, or as some say, good guilt and bad guilt. *Being* guilty differs from *feeling* guilty. Guilt is the state of having done a wrong or committed an offense. This is guilt as defined by theologians. But guilt also is the painful feeling of self-reproach resulting from doing wrong—guilt as defined by psychologists.

Real guilt feelings result when we have done wrong. False guilt, however, seizes us when we believe we have done something wrong when, in fact, we have done nothing wrong.

True guilt keeps people in line by acting as an internal alarm that warns us of danger. False guilt, however, keeps the alarm ringing even after we've been notified of the problem or even when there is no danger.

The point is that we do not need to give in indiscriminately to all of our feelings of guilt. If our guilt alarm is false, we need to turn it off and go on with life. But many of us run into trouble when we try to dismantle our false guilt. Like a car alarm triggered when the owner is away, false alarms go on and on and on. In fact, the ring is so persistent that it often makes people behave as though the guilt were real. That can be especially harmful to a marriage.

After a decade of research on the emotion of guilt, I (Les) discovered that feeling guilty sabotages our ability to empathize. And empathy is critical to the health of a marriage; it's the ability to objectively understand your mate's perspective and see the world from his or her point of view. But when guilt enters the picture, it clouds our vision. We become self-absorbed and can't put ourselves in our partner's shoes. Guilt is a self-centered emotion that seeps into the crevices of our marriage and does its work in ways we aren't even aware of. I call it "love's unseen enemy."

So if you find that guilt has wormed its way into your relationship, ask yourself if it is real or false. If it is real, ask for and receive forgiveness. Don't grovel in self-punishment to somehow prove your innocence. Accept your human frailty and do whatever you can to make it right. Then rely on God's strength to help you regain respect and move on. If your guilt is false, recognize it as such and disregard your unhealthy feelings. Look at the situation objectively and face the future with hope.

Don't allow the poison of guilt to ruin your marriage. Don't allow it to gain a foothold and keep you from empathizing with each other. Instead, remember that there is no condemnation for those who are in Christ Jesus (Romans 8).

I know marriage is serious business, but sometimes we get so intense about our relationship that it almost takes the fun out of it. How can we lighten up and bring more humor into our marriage?

We've always worked hard at not being too serious in our marriage. And it's paid off. Humor has saved us on many occasions from allowing disappointing circumstances to ruin valuable time together. Whether it be uncooperative weather, a rude waiter, or not being able to find a parking space on the day of a fun outing, humor has often been our saving grace. And on occasion, it has saved us from our own, self-created debacles. Not that we consistently agree on what is funny, but the longer we are married, the more we tend to laugh at the same things. Allow us to share a few of the lessons we have learned about bringing more humor into marriage.

First of all, humor is always risky. What is appealing to some is appalling to others. In a survey of over 14,000 *Psychology Today* readers who rated thirty jokes, the findings were unequivocal. "Every single joke," it was reported, "had a substantial number of fans who rated it 'very funny,' while another group dismissed it as 'not at all funny.'" Apparently, our funny bones are located in different places. Some laugh uproariously at the slapstick of Larry, Mo, and Curly, while others enjoy the more cerebral humor of Woody Allen.

Whatever you and your spouse find funny, don't neglect it. Humor can serve as a healing balm to the tough times your marriage encounters. Humor helps us cope—not just with the trivial but even with the tragic. Psychoanalyst Martin Grotjahn, author of *Beyond Laughter*, notes that "to have a sense of humor is to have an understanding of human suffering." Charlie Chaplin could have said the same thing. Chaplin grew up in the poorest section of London. His mother suffered from serious mental illness and his father died of alcoholism when Charlie was just five. Laughter was Chaplin's tool for coping with life's losses. Chaplin's eating a boiled leather shoe for dinner in his classic film *Gold Rush* is more than a humorous scene. It is an act of human triumph, a monument to the coping power of humor.

One does not need to be a professional comedian, however, to benefit from comedy. Viktor Frankl is another example of how humor can empower a person to contend with horrendous circumstances. In Frankl's book *Man's Search for Meaning*, he speaks of using humor to survive imprisonment during World War II. Frankl and another inmate would invent at least one amusing story daily to help them cope with their horrors.

"If you can find humor in anything," according to Bill Cosby, "you can survive it." Researchers agree. Studies reveal that individuals who have a strong sense of humor are less likely to experience depression and other emotional struggles.

So strengthen your marital bond with a little humor. Look for incongruities that both of you can laugh at. Pascal and Kant were some of the first to regard humor as essentially a sudden unrelated shift in our thinking. Mark Twain provided an example when he said, "Cauliflower is nothing but cabbage with a college education." The incongruity of a vegetable being educated is humorous. Dick Van Dyke falling over an ottoman in his living room is funny because our momentary confusion is transformed into an appreciation for the joke. We laugh when the unstable structure in the humor becomes stable, and we "get the point."

You might also want to relieve a little tension with humor. Sigmund Freud, who described humor as a "rare and precious gift," postulated the tension relief theory. He saw humor as an opportunity to release stress built up in our overly rational and demanding world. At one point during the Cuban missile crisis, Soviet and American negotiators became deadlocked. They sat in silence until one of the Russians told a riddle: "What is the difference between capitalism and communism?" The answer? "In capitalism, people exploit people. In communism, it's the other way around." Humor relieves stress. So even when the two of you are uptight, look for some levity.

Recalling times when you laughed together is also a way of bringing more humor to the present. An embarrassing moment or a line from a movie or sitcom that struck you funny can be retold again and again. Not long ago, we were stressed out and under pressure to get our home clean for guests. In the midst of the tension, Leslie repeated a line that an exasperated apartment manager said to us long ago in our very first apartment. The statement would mean nothing to anyone else, but it makes us laugh. Recalling times like this can go a long way in bringing levity back to your marriage.

"A person without a sense of humor," according to the American minister Henry Ward Beecher, "is like a wagon without springs—jolted by every pebble in the road." By finding the humor in your partnering predicaments you will make marriage a much smoother ride.

My wife says I never express my feelings, and I say she has enough emotions for the both of us. We genuinely want to understand each other, but often get tangled up in the different ways we each express our feelings. Can you help?

Too often in marriage we take for granted that our spouse should know exactly how we are feeling. But that's unfair. Feelings are too fickle and unpredictable to put that burden on another person. The following strategies can help you express your feelings in a way that will allow your spouse to truly understand them.

1. *Use "I" statements.* If your spouse is to accurately understand your feelings, it will be because you, first of all, take responsibility for your feelings by using "I" statements rather than "you" statements. Notice how blaming these "you" statements sound:

"You make me furious."

"You're driving me crazy."

"You never let me get a word in."

If you recast these same statements by taking responsibility for them, they become less inflammatory and are much more likely to be heard:

"I'm furious."

"I feel confused and crazy."

"I want to talk now."

Of course, just because a statement begins with "I" doesn't mean that it is a legitimate "I" statement; for example, "I feel that you are a jerk."

2. *Be honest.* It is tempting to describe dinner with your in-laws as "fine, very pleasant," when actually you were bored and irritated the whole evening. It is tempting to say that you're tired and just want to go to bed when actually you are worried about the finances and afraid to broach the subject. But as hard as this may be, resist the temptation. When you cut your partner off from your true feelings, you also cut yourself off and make it that much harder to genuinely express emotions.

3. *Be congruent.* It's very confusing when your tone of voice and body language don't match your words. If you say "I'm not angry" while your tight face communicates the contrary, which is your partner supposed to believe, your words or your nonverbal behavior? So if you notice that your body language is incongruent with your statements, this may indicate that you actually

do feel differently about the topic than you think you do. Spend some time looking inside and see how you really feel. On the other hand, you may just have developed a habit of smiling when you deliver bad news or frowning when joking or some other incongruent style. If necessary, practice in front of a mirror until your posture, tone of voice, gestures, and so on match the way you feel. This may feel strange, but it may also bring you that much closer to expressing your feelings so that your spouse hears and accurately understands them.

Once we got married, I thought I would never feel alone again. I mean, my husband is my soul mate, my best friend, and we have each other. But why do I sometimes still feel lonely?

Feeling alone and neglected is becoming an emotional epidemic in America. Loneliness—the painful awareness that we are not meaningfully connected to others—floods the lives of millions. It is one of "the most universal sources of human suffering."[12] And if you thought that getting married would automatically protect you from this dreaded feeling, you could not be more wrong. Countless couples in married relationships suffer from loneliness.

The question begs to be asked: Why? Why would a person in a committed, loving relationship experience loneliness? The answer may not be what you want to hear, but it's true. Loneliness is often the result of protecting oneself against rejection. Even in marriage, we can erect a wall that prevents our true self from being seen and accepted. We reason that if we are not vulnerable, our partner cannot reject our real selves. Such self-defeating attitudes usually stem from experiences of rejection as children. When this is the case, one's ability to trust other people—even a spouse— has been damaged and must be restored.

Rebuilding the kind of trust that diminishes loneliness begins with gaining the courage to risk authenticity. It begins by disclosing your real feelings. That means turning off the television and other distractions to have a meaningful heart-to-heart talk about what's going on with both of you.

Another reason for loneliness in marriage is a misbelief that says my partner should meet all of my emotional needs. The truth is that no human being can do this. If you are expecting them to, you are doomed to disappointment and loneliness. The solution is to find friendship with God. Within each of us is a God-shaped void, an emptiness that can only be filled by a relationship with God himself. Until we find our connection with God, we will always suffer twinges of loneliness. Jesus has promised never to leave us or forsake us (see Matthew 28:20). He hears us when we pray. His Holy Spirit comes to us as the Comforter.

Marriage is a place of great solace, but it cannot compare to the ultimate comfort that comes only through a relationship with God. So don't suffer silently in loneliness because you thought marriage was to supposed to "cure" all painful feelings. Instead, talk to your mate about your feelings and talk to God too.

What are some of the most helpful resources on handling emotions in marriage?

Unlocking the Mystery of Your Emotions by Archibald Hart (Word, 1989).

> Many people either lose control of their emotions (creating pain and chaos) or overcontrol them (becoming stunted, distant, and cold). This book shows you how to experience emotions fully without letting them get out of hand. With balanced professionalism, biblical integrity, and down-to-earth practicality, Dr. Hart shows how you can learn to be "real" instead of perfect.

Love's Unseen Enemy: How to Overcome Guilt to Build Healthy Relationships by Les Parrott III (Zondervan, 1994).

Too often efforts to build a loving marriage are unwittingly sabotaged by an unseen enemy: guilt. This book shows how to build a healthy relationship by overcoming the feelings of false guilt and by dealing forthrightly with true guilt. It identifies four relationship styles created by the combination of love and guilt: Pleaser, Controller, Withholder, and Lover.

Love and Anger in Marriage by David Mace (Zondervan, 1982).

World-renowned marriage counselor David Mace believes that many people have totally overlooked the positive functions anger can perform for them—even in close, intimate relationships like marriage. Mace demonstrates the interaction that takes place between a couple as their relationship grows and develops through the many love-anger cycles that arise in daily living together. This honest book will bring new life and hope to many angry marriages.

Chapter Five:
Questions About Gender

I hear a lot of talk about how men and women have different needs, and I am the first to admit it's true. However, I have a tough time trying to pinpoint these needs so that I can better understand my wife. I think she feels the same way about me. Can you help?

While "birds of a feather flock together," sometimes things that go together are very different: bacon and eggs or a violin and a bow. The same could be said of a man and woman coming together in marriage. Two halves becoming one whole.

Every cell of our bodies, as men and women, differ. The skeletal structure, for example, of women is shorter and broader. Women's blood contains fewer red cells, making them tire more easily. Women have a larger stomach, kidneys, liver, and appendix, but smaller lungs. Scores of other physical differences may influence the way each person in marriage feels and behaves. But in addition to the more obvious physical differences between the genders, societal expectations and modeling contribute to a plethora of differences between the sexes—all culminating in several gender-specific unique needs.

Many marital problems evolve because men try to meet needs that they would value and women do the same. The problem is that since the needs of men and women are often so different, we waste effort trying to meet the wrong needs. If we are truly committed to valuing our life partners, we must not only understand and appreciate our partner's differences, but we must commit ourselves to meeting their unique needs.

Willard F. Harley, in his popular book *His Needs, Her Needs*, has given us a great tool to do just that.[1] He identifies the ten most important marital needs of husbands and wives. You may or may not agree with all of them, but they can serve as a good discussion starter:

She needs affection. It symbolizes security, protection, comfort, and approval. A hug expresses affection. And for the typical wife, there can hardly be enough of them.

He needs sexual fulfillment. Just as women crave affection, so men want sex. And they don't just want their wives to make their bodies available. They need to feel their wife is as invested in sex as they are.

She needs conversation. Not just talk about her husband's problems or achievements, but about her problems and her hopes. She needs quality conversation on a daily basis.

He needs recreational companionship. After sex, the need for recreation rates highest for men. He needs time spent in a mutually satisfying activity—whether it be sports, shopping, cooking, painting, etc.

She needs honesty and openness. Mistrust destroys a woman's marital security. If a husband does not keep up honest communication with his wife, he eventually undermines her trust and destroys any hope of security.

He needs an attractive spouse. A man does not need a supermodel for a wife, but he wants her to make an effort to be attractive to him. He wants her to dress in clothes he likes and do her hair in a style that is appealing to him.

She needs financial support. A husband's failure to provide sufficient income sends shudders through the underpinnings of a marriage. A woman needs to know that her husband is taking care of their family's needs and their future.

He needs domestic support. Old-fashioned or not, most men fantasize about a loving, pleasant home where few hassles occur and life runs smoothly.

She needs family commitment. Wives want their husbands to take a strong role in the marriage and express how important it is to them. They need to see evidence of a strong commitment to family life that is not overshadowed by work or anything else.

He needs admiration. Honest admiration is a great motivator for most men. When a woman tells her husband (who has been sweating it out at work) she thinks he's wonderful, that inspires him and keeps him going.

Like we said, you may not agree with all of these "needs," but the number of people who have bought and read Harley's book (more than 250,000) is enough reason to take them seriously and discuss how each of your particular sets of needs differs.

Remember, if you commit yourself to meeting the unique needs of your partner, you will become irresistible to each other and insure faithfulness in your marriage. You will build a relationship that sustains romance, increases intimacy, and deepens awareness year after year.

Sometimes it feels like we are speaking different languages. What I think I said isn't what he heard and vice versa. Maybe if I knew just how men and women communicate differently, I could do something about it. What are the differences in communication between men and women?

Only recently have researchers begun to understand the drastic difference in how men and women communicate. Deborah Tannen and other sociolinguists have come to believe that the genders speak so differently, in fact, that they can be considered different languages—or at least different "genderlects."[2]

In her groundbreaking book *You Just Don't Understand*, Tannen suggests that men grow up in a competitive world. To men, life is a challenge, a confrontation, a struggle to preserve independence and avoid failure, a contest in which they strive to be one up on their colleagues. In their conversations, men attempt to establish power and status. In the world of status, *independence* is the key.

Women, on the other hand, approach the world seeking connection and intimacy, close friendships, and equality with their friends. In their conversations, they try to give confirmation and support and to reach consensus. For women, *intimacy* is the key in the world of connection.

If women emphasize connections and intimacy and men emphasize independence and status, conflicts and misunderstandings are bound to arise. For example, many women feel it is natural to consult their partner at every turn, while men automatically make more decisions without consultation. Women expect decisions to be discussed first and to be made by consensus. They appreciate discussion itself as evidence of involvement and caring. But many men feel oppressed by lengthy discussions about what they see as minor decisions. They feel restrained if they can't act without a lot of talking first. Women may try to invite a free-wheeling conversation by asking, "What do you think?" Men may take the question literally and think they are being asked to make a decision when in reality their partner only wants conversation.

For many men who work in competitive positions, the comfort of home means freedom from having to prove themselves and impress others through verbal display. At last, they are in a situation where talk is not required and they are free to remain silent. But for a woman, home is the place where she and her partner are free to talk. Especially for the traditional housewife, the return of her husband from work means they can talk, interact, and be intimate. In this situation, the woman is likely to take her husband's silence as a rejection while he takes her need to talk as an invasion of his privacy.

Although the communication styles of men and women differ in many respects, it is a mistake to think that one style is better than the other. What is important is to learn how to interpret each other's messages and explain your own in a way your partner can accept. There's no one right way to listen, to talk, or to have a conversation. Although a woman may focus more often on intimacy and rapport and her partner more on status, this difference need not lead to misunderstanding if the couple accepts that such differences do not imply that one partner's communication style is correct and the other's is wrong.

I'm embarrassed to admit that my wife's period is pretty much of a mystery to me. For example, I don't know why it is never regular. I'm sure if I understood it better I would understand her more. As a man, what should I know about my wife's menstrual cycle?

A woman's menstrual cycle involves the series of hormonal changes that prepare a woman's body for possible pregnancy during each month of her reproductive years. There are four phases in the menstrual cycle: the follicular phase (during which one or more eggs begin to mature), ovulation (when the egg is released from the follicle), the luteal phase (during which the egg-releasing follicle continues to make hormones that affect the woman's cycle), and menstruation (during which menstrual fluid is released).

The length of the menstrual cycle varies from woman to woman and from cycle to cycle. Some women have 20-day cycles while others have cycles lasting 40 days. And the same woman might have a 32-day cycle one month and a 27-day cycle the next. Stress, illness, nutrition, and changes in routine can affect the release of hormones and thus the length of the cycle. Menstruation occurs only if no fertilized egg has been implanted. The menstrual period, lasting two to six days, is set off by a sharp fall in estrogen and progesterone levels.

Understanding the basic biology of my wife's menstrual cycle is one thing, but coping with PMS is another. What advice do you have for how couples should handle premenstrual syndrome?

For one week each month, Linda experienced an emotional and physical upheaval that built, like trapped steam, to an explosion the day before her period began. She became forgetful, clumsy, irritated, and short with people. Severe physical symptoms, including bloating and breast pain, compounded her emotional distress. And the person she loved the most—her husband—often bore the brunt of her monthly outbursts. Indeed, Linda's severe premenstrual syndrome threatened to ruin her marriage.

Then she got help. Her physician put her on a program that included physical exercise. To her surprise, Linda discovered that exercise reduced the irritability, insomnia, and moodiness she experienced each month just before her period. "Exercise is not something I just do for me, I need to do it for my marriage," she told us in a counseling session.

Regular workouts are just one new prescription for the ever-controversial premenstrual syndrome (PMS), the physical and/or emotional changes that complicate the lives of seventy percent of women each month at some point during the two weeks prior to their periods.

At one time physicians and many husbands assumed that PMS was "all in the heads" of the women who complained of monthly symptoms. Thankfully, this incorrect attitude is slowly changing. Premenstrual conditions are being taken more seriously, and researchers have identified three types, all with varying levels of severity. A *premenstrual change*, the mildest form, affects about a quarter of all women; *premenstrual syndrome*, the moderate form, is the most common; and *premenstrual dysphoric disorder* (PDD), the worst kind, strikes three to eight percent of all women. To be diagnosed with any of these, a woman must experience symptoms consistently during the two weeks prior to her period.

Women who experience a premenstrual change have one physical symptom, such as bloating. Premenstrual syndrome is defined by the presence of two or more symptoms, such as breast tenderness, water retention, and headaches. About half of the women with the syndrome also experience mood changes (irritability, for example), but not to the extent that their daily lives are disrupted. Women with premenstrual dysphoric disorder, on the other hand, experience many symptoms, including lethargy, mood change, insomnia, or a change in appetite. These symptoms must be so severe that they disrupt a woman's life.

Experts recommend that women chart their premenstrual symptoms with a doctor's supervision for at least two months. This will help determine the severity of symptoms, and once diagnosed, a physician can then find the most effective way to manage the symptoms. For women with a premenstrual change or PMS, working out and eating a diet high in complex carbohydrates are recommended. These activities prompt chemical reactions that help boost serotonin levels in the brain. For women suffering from PDD, medication may be the answer.

Unfortunately, there is no cure for every premenstrual problem. But now, millions of women who until recently had no choice but to suffer, can manage their symptoms more effectively. And that can make for a much happier marriage.

Perhaps the most important thing you can do as husband and wife to ease this monthly stress is to work as a team. Adjust chores, rearrange schedules if needed. Do what you can do together to make it easier. Of course, this means that you must talk about how the symptoms are affecting your marriage.

If PMS stress continues to interfere with your day-to-day activities and your marriage, however, it's time to seek help. Call your local hospital's departments of obstetrics and gynecology, psychology and psychiatry. There are now too many effective ways to manage PMS so it doesn't manage your marriage.

What are some of the most helpful resources on gender and marriage?

His Needs, Her Needs: Building an Affair-Proof Marriage by Willard F. Harley, Jr. (Fleming H. Revell, 1986).

Harley writes with a conviction that couples need to learn how to care for each other by understanding fundamental gender differences. Once a spouse understands his or her partner's unique needs, the process of trying to meet those needs can begin. Harley shows you how to become "irresistible" to each other and avoid the common errors that lead to affairs and divorce.

Men & Women: Enjoying the Difference by Larry Crabb (Zondervan, 1991).

Giving numerous examples from his counseling and speaking ministry, Crabb explores how we can turn away from ourselves and toward each other, how we can consider our mate's needs and become what he calls "other centered." He maintains that men and women are different in important ways that, if understood and honored, can lead to a deep enjoyment of one another, an enjoyment that can last forever.

You Just Don't Understand: Women and Men in Conversation by Deborah Tannen (Ballantine, 1990).

Professor of linguistics Dr. Tannen provides a readable account of the complexities of communication between men and women. What she is saying is that men and women grow up in such profoundly different ways, and see themselves connecting to each other in such profoundly different ways, that the two sexes are really trying to communicate across two different cultures. This book goes a long way toward helping couples speak the same language.

CHAPTER SIX:
QUESTIONS ABOUT IN-LAWS

We both come from loving homes that, more or less, support our relationship. But in the few months that we have been married, the infamous "in-law" issue has appeared on the horizon. We haven't had a major blowout or anything, but I'm becoming increasingly fearful. Are conflicts with in-laws inevitable?

Someone once observed that Adam and Eve got along as well as they did because neither had any in-laws to worry about. Maybe so, but they still had plenty of problems to deal with. Problems are a part of life, and while in-laws may add to them, they can also lighten the load.

Ask around. Some couples couldn't be happier about their in-laws, while other couples feel that their in-laws are the source of most of their problems. If you tend to identify more with the latter group, don't think you are alone. Experts believe that three-quarters of all married couples have problems with their in-laws.[1]

Some of the most common in-law problems include keeping a son-in-law or daughter-in-law at a distance, giving them the cold shoulder, and treating them as a person who has invaded the family or is not good enough for their son or daughter. Another common in-law problem is gift-giving with strings attached. This occurs when they offer some kind of help (monetary or otherwise) and then treat it as a license to tell you exactly how to use it. Of course, criticism is also a major in-law complaint by couples. Some in-laws constantly critique each and every choice a couple makes. And yet another in-law problem appears when they intrude on one's marriage when they are not welcome. They may smother and hover over the marriage without making room for the couple to have privacy.

If you do not identify with any of these problems or others related to in-laws, count yourself fortunate and in the minority. Most couples struggle to some degree or another with issues related to their partner's parents.

By the way, one of the most surprising difficulties many newlyweds have with their in-laws is knowing how to address them. In the early years of marriage, many couples simply avoid calling their in-laws by name, and this can create tension. So if you have not yet settled this issue, put it out on the table. Simply ask your in-laws how they would like to be addressed by you— by first names, "Mom and Dad," or what? Once decided, use their names often. Spend time with them and take an interest in their work, hobbies, ideas, and experiences. Knowing them better will make for a much easier relationship.

We've been married five years and every Thanksgiving, Christmas, or Easter we have a huge debate over whose home we should go to. More than once it has taken the joy out of the celebration. What advice can you give us on how to decide whose home to go to for the holidays?

Most couples, especially newlyweds, expect the holidays to be a perfect opportunity for bringing them closer together as they celebrate the season as husband and wife. Unfortunately, the "happiest time of the year" often turns out to be one of the toughest on marriages.

If choosing how to meld two families' holiday traditions were not enough for most couples, there is the quandary of whose home each holiday will be devoted to. If both families have strong

Christmas traditions, for example, each one expects you to spend the season with them. And since geography usually prevents you from splitting your time, there is bound to be disappointment and hurt feelings one way or the other. However, there are some practical things you can do to make this situation easier on everyone involved:

1. *Admit the potential for problems.* The first step in creating a happy holiday for both of you is to be open with each other about the possibility of hitting some turbulence. If you try to ignore it, the problems will only become bigger. So think through how things might go and how each family might respond. Then share your different perspectives, just the two of you, in a calm and compassionate atmosphere.

2. *Make plans early.* Acknowledging the potential for family disputes isn't enough. If the first step to handling such problems is recognizing their likelihood, the second step is establishing a plan of action. If both families are expecting you to join them for the holidays, for example, start making your plans in the early fall. This gives everyone time to adjust their feelings and will make for a much smoother long-term ride for the two of you.

3. *Give and take without being finicky.* You will only complicate your problem if you do not avail yourself of old-fashioned flexibility and compromise. It may help to trade off Thanksgiving at your house for Christmas at your partner's. Or maybe this year will be spent with your partner's family and next year with yours. The point is to be open to suggestions and compromise.

4. *Be careful how you compromise.* Sometimes couples get caught in the trap of trying to please everyone but themselves. It is important that you focus on making your holiday special for the two of you and not just your families. For example, if your families live just hours apart, you might be considering splitting your time on Christmas Day between them. But think about spending most of that special day en route from one house to the

other. Is that really what you want? If not, be sure you adjust your expectations accordingly.

5. *Be loyal to each other.* This is critically important. As you break the news to the parents who won't be seeing you around the holidays this year, take great care not to blame your partner or your in-laws for the situation. Let your parents know that this is a decision you've made together as a team. This is important because if your parents get the idea you are being "forced" to do something you really don't want to do, they may feel compelled to get involved.

6. *Align your attitude to be positive even when things turn negative.* If you are to make it through the holidays successfully balancing both families, it will not be because you have perfect circumstances—that simply does not happen. Circumstances will always complicate our plans and hopes. But by adjusting to circumstances beyond your control with a positive outlook, you will take huge leaps forward in creating a wonderful family holiday.

7. *Keep in mind the reason for the season.* Take time to remember the true meaning of Christmas. Remember that God created everything the season is about: Jesus, giving, goodwill, and love. As you think on these things, you will gain a bigger perspective than simply trying to negotiate your time.

These guidelines are not guaranteed to take away every ounce of turmoil associated with trying to work out a happy holiday for everyone in your immediate and extended family, but they can help you make the whole process a bit easier.

When my spouse and I meet with his family, he completely ignores me. I mean it's like I'm not even at the dinner table. He isn't mean or degrading, it's just that all of his attention is on his family, not me. On the drive home from his parents' house the last time this happened, I brought it to his attention and he didn't even know what I was talking about. What can I do to improve this situation?

We've struggled with this same problem ourselves. It used to be that whenever we went to Les's home, he shifted into premarriage mode and forgot I was his wife. Rarely checking in with me, he'd go visit his buddies, take off with his dad, and so on—leaving me to fend for myself. He didn't mean to do it, but it felt like I was invisible, a mere tagalong at best. And it felt terribly lonely. Thank goodness, things changed. Let me tell you how we resolved this problem.

First of all, after I noticed how predictable this pattern was becoming, I spoke up. In private, I asked Les if he realized what was happening and, like your husband, he didn't. He was having a good time at home and just assumed I was too. I can understand that, and I was careful not to blame him or lash out because I felt wounded. However, I told him how I was feeling, and he began to see the situation from my perspective. This would have never happened if I had accused him of deliberately ignoring me (that is guaranteed to lead to a defensive position and solve nothing). But by focusing on what was going on inside me when he took off without my input or didn't include me in discussions, I helped him put himself in my shoes. And it worked.

Next, I asked him for his perspective on what it was like for him to be at his family's home. He hadn't really given it much thought before my question, but soon confessed that being home caused him to regress a bit to a more carefree time. He simply enjoyed the fun of being a "kid" and not having to worry about much of anything. This discussion helped me not to take his behavior personally, as I was tempted to do. Anyway, the lights went on for him when he realized how this kind of mode made me feel left out.

As we talked more about it, we devised a very simple action plan together. This included, at Les's suggestion, a commitment on his part to include me in discussions and keep me informed of what he was up to. I suggested that I would bring a book for times when he wanted to go off with his dad or somebody else.

But one of the most important parts of our action plan was to have a few secret signals only the two of us would know about. Quietly touching our partner's elbow or even making simple eye contact, for example, became our way of staying in touch (we'll keep the messages to ourselves, thank you). It became our own marriage "Morse code," and after years of being together we still use it in a variety of settings. We have a signal that means "rescue me." I've used this more than once at his home when I was on my third round of Monopoly with his nephews.

One more component of our action plan which helped me tremendously was a conscious effort on Les's part to touch me more often. A gentle squeeze on the shoulder as he was walking by or holding my hand every so often was key to letting me know I mattered and that I was not being ignored.

We do not have the definitive answer on this problem, but this little plan has worked well for us and a few couples we have shared it with. Try it yourselves. Have a frank but gentle discussion about how you are feeling, invite him to discuss his experience, and then devise your own plan of action to correct the problem.

My in-laws are not friendly people to begin with, but there is no mistaking the fact that they did not give their blessing to our marriage. I had this fantasy that after we got married they would come around, but they haven't. What can I do if my in-laws don't accept me?

The stress of trying to bond with in-laws who treat you like an outlaw can render family get-togethers painfully miserable.

If you or your partner find it difficult to mesh with the in-laws, you need to ask yourself why. If, for example, you feel like an outsider around your partner's family, ask yourself if there is something you're doing or saying that's holding them back. Then ask yourself what you can do to win them over. Would it help to have some one-on-one time with your partner's mom or dad? Are you doing something that might be perceived as threatening (e.g., breaking an unspoken family rule)? Are your aspirations not what they hoped for? If so, maybe it would help to talk openly and calmly with your in-laws about it. Of course, the trick is not to get defensive if you broach the subject. Work at understanding them rather than being understood by them.

If your best efforts to win them over seem to come up empty, it may be time for your partner to intervene and find out what's bothering your in-laws. If you go this route, however, your spouse must make his or her loyalty to you known to them. This helps prevent an emotional triangle from being formed. An emotional triangle is where one person is invariably caught in the middle, being used by the other two parties to send messages. And you certainly don't want that. If your spouse feels caught in the middle because he or she is trying to ride the fence, your marriage will weaken and your frustration will compound. Besides, presenting a united front shows them that you are really in love and that their child makes you happy. They may then realize that if their child loves you, perhaps they should, too.

Once you have made every effort to win your partner's parents over, the issue has been put on the table and opened for discussion, and your in-laws are still not embracing you, it is time to shift gears. At this point, you need to begin thinking with your partner about how to maintain your own sense of well-being within this relationship. That may require setting some boundaries.

For example, you may need to set limits on how often you and your partner get together with the in-laws. While this may be difficult for your partner, he or she needs to realize that bonding with you may mean risking a more distant relationship with parents. And more than likely, the parents who were once distant will gain more respect for you and your marriage. You might even see the relations with your in-laws improve as you work at maintaining your own well-being.

When you get married, your spouse's family becomes an extension of your own. And pleasing two sets of parents, as well as your mate, can prove difficult for a new bride or groom. The bottom line, however, is that you can only do so much to "make somebody like you." After you have done your best and given it a little time, it becomes their problem, not yours.

My in-laws are very sweet people and I appreciate all their kindness, but sometimes they become so involved in our lives that it drives me nuts. What can I do when my in-laws smother us?

While the problem of trying to build a relationship with disengaged or distant in-laws is troublesome, it may seem like a welcome relief to the married couple who is trying to cope with parents who are constantly nosing their way into their marriage.

Winston Churchill's "darling Clementine" learned early that she had married not just her husband but his strong-willed mother as well. When she and Winston returned from their honeymoon, the young bride discovered that Lady Randolph Churchill had completely redecorated the couple's new home in a style far fancier than Clementine had planned.

If you can relate to Clementine, you are not alone. Smothering in-laws affect a significant number of marriages. Even if you don't live under the same roof with your in-laws—or even in the same time zone—daily phone calls and frequent visits can make it seem like they are living in the next room.

One of the most common reasons some in-laws smother a marriage is because they feel like they have a right to. Where would such an idea come from, you ask? Usually from a financial string that keeps them tightly tied to you. So if you are feeling smothered, it may be because you have not yet unhooked yourself financially. Of course, the indebtedness may not be only financial. It could be that you are relying on Mom and Dad for regular child care because it is convenient and cheap. However, this kind of favor is not always as "cheap" as you might think. So consider why your in-laws might feel that they have a right to meddle in your marriage and then do something to change it.

Another important consideration is setting boundaries with your domineering in-laws. When they intrude, speak up. Let them know that you need some private time or space. Be polite but assertive. Don't feel obligated to offer explanations or apologize for your needs. Simply state your request and stick to it. If, for example, they are expecting you to be at their home for Thanksgiving, never asking you for your input on the decision, you might say, "We have discussed it and decided together that this year we are going to celebrate Thanksgiving in our own home. You are welcome to join us if you wish." This kind of decision lets your in-laws know that they cannot make up your mind for you, and it still allows them to be included in your life.

As you set your boundaries with in-laws, take care not to throw out the good with the bad. Sure, their nosy behavior gets under your skin. Of course, you don't appreciate their intrusions. But consider the good they bring to your relationship. Appreciate and respect them for who they are. As you keep an eye out for the good, it will help you swallow the bad more easily.

Along these same lines, accept that your in-laws, like any other human beings, are imperfect. They aren't likely to change radically at this point in their lives. So gain some tolerance for their nosy ways by learning more about them. In fact it is a great diversion to ask them about their childhood, their courtship, their hobbies, and so on. Along the way you will probably gain some insights into their present behavior. Who knows, you might even end up *asking* them for their wisdom!

What are some of the most helpful resources on coping with in-law issues and marriage?

The Other Woman in Your Marriage by H. Norman Wright (Regal, 1994).

It should be no surprise that the powerful bond between a mother and son puts pressure on many marriages. "When a man's relationship with his mother is so powerful," asks Norm Wright, "is there any room for his wife?" This book is dedicated to helping wives find peace in the midst of the mother-son-wife triangle. It takes a close look at this in-law relationship and helps couples establish healthy boundaries as well as open lines of communication. Read it and make peace with "the other woman."

Boundaries: When to Say Yes, When to Say No, to Take Control of Your Life by Henry Cloud and John Townsend (Zondervan, 1992).

Having clear boundaries is essential to a healthy relationship with in-laws. A boundary is a personal property line that marks those things for which we are responsible. In other words, boundaries define who we are. In this best-selling book, Cloud and Townsend describe the importance of physical boundaries, mental boundaries, emotional boundaries, and spiritual boundaries. While this book is not written solely about setting boundaries with in-laws, many of its principles can be applied to this relationship.

In-laws, Outlaws: How to Make Peace with His Family and Yours by Penny Bilofsky and Fredda Sacharow (New York: Villard Books, 1991).

This book points the way to skills needed to understand, intercept, and solve nearly every type of in-law problem. Readers learn how to master good interpersonal communication, set limits and boundaries, adjust their own expectations to reality, and recognize core issues rather than respond to the immediate situation. With step-by-step instructions, the book addresses issues such as meeting your in-laws for the first time, planning the wedding, when children arrive (or don't), holidays and family gatherings, and reaching out to sibling in-laws.

Chapter Seven:
Questions About Intimacy

I hear a lot about the importance of intimacy for building a successful marriage, and I'd like to know whether we have much of it in our relationship. However, I'm not so sure I really know what intimacy is. Could you explain or define intimacy for me?

An intimate relationship, in its simplest form, is simply being close. It is the opposite of distance or standing apart. Intimacy involves a sharing and uncovering of selves. The word *intimate* is derived from the Latin word *intimus*, meaning "inmost." Couples who are intimate tell one another their private thoughts, dreams, insecurities, and triumphs; they know a great deal about one another. Lillian Rubin, author of *Intimate Strangers*, expresses it this way: "Intimacy is some kind of reciprocal expression of feeling and thought, not out of fear or dependent need, but out of a wish to know another's inner life and to be able to share one's own."[1]

An intimate relationship is a committed relationship. The partners involved in it are committed to one another's well-being. Intimate couples trust one another and are willing to make sacrifices for one another. One way of summing up the intimate relationship is to say that it is the epitome of empathy. Partners in an intimate marriage have an ability to feel what the other is feeling and know what he or she is needing.

To measure intimacy, social scientists ask individuals involved in relationships a variety of questions. The following are sample questions from an intimacy scale you might be interested in answering.[2]

1. When you have leisure time, how often do you choose to spend it with your spouse?

   Very Rarely   Some of the Time   Almost Always
   1   2   3   4   5   6   7   8   9   10

2. How often do you show your spouse affection?

   Very Rarely   Some of the Time   Almost Always
   1   2   3   4   5   6   7   8   9   10

3. How often do you confide very personal information to your spouse?

   Very Rarely   Some of the Time   Almost Always
   1   2   3   4   5   6   7   8   9   10

4. How often are you able to understand your spouse's feelings?

   Very Rarely   Some of the Time   Almost Always
   1   2   3   4   5   6   7   8   9   10

5. How often do you feel close to your spouse?

   Very Rarely   Some of the Time   Almost Always
   1   2   3   4   5   6   7   8   9   10

These questions help us tap into the intensity of our intimacy. The higher your score, the stronger your current feelings of intimacy with your partner. Of course, intimacy is not a constant. There are times when intimacy is stronger and times that it fades. But for committed married couples, intimacy is a top priority, and they take the time to cultivate it.

If we want more intimacy in our marriage, what is the most important thing we can be doing?

We tend to think of love and intimacy on a grand scale—for better, for worse; till death do us part—and we associate it with life's big moments. We plan birthday parties, produce holiday celebrations, and get romantic on anniversaries. These loving gestures help maintain a marriage because they acknowledge the importance of your relationship. But there's another kind of acknowledgment, requiring far less effort, that can pay even larger dividends: It's the small affectionate gesture.

Quick: What were the first words you said to your spouse this morning? If they were along the lines of "Where are my socks?" or "You left the hall light on again," rather than something affectionate, it's time to remind yourself of the importance of small affectionate gestures. These are the sweet "Good mornings" and the gentle cuddlings under the comforter that express affection. These are the little building blocks of intimacy.

Why is it that so many couples neglect affectionate gestures? Mostly because they have become too comfortable with each other—taking each other for granted.

There are specific gestures intimate couples use and estranged couples don't. For example, loving couples speak sweetly to each other. They may clash, sometimes fiercely, but researchers have identified a pattern to their behavior: Roughly five positive things are said for every unpleasant one.[3] These couples have a general sense that the good outweighs the bad. They don't use phony flattery to make up for negative words. They genuinely express kindness.

Intimacy is also built on conversations filled with supportive questions, tag questions such as "Do you agree?" and "What do you think?" Little questions like these open the conversation to the other person's views.

One of the most important things a couple can do to build intimacy is to intentionally reconnect after being apart. This is accomplished with a small gesture of support that says "It's good to see you." It is communicated not in words, but with the eyes. We all know how good it feels to walk into someone's presence and have them look up and smile, and how awful it is if he or she is preoccupied or negative. This kind of preoccupation dampens kindness and suffocates intimacy.

Underlying every affectionate gesture, no matter how small, is respect. Grand gestures on significant occasions mark the passage of time. But little gestures that sweeten the moment show respect. In these moments we discover the heart of intimacy and feel the warmth of a loving connection.

I felt close to my husband on our honeymoon, but in the last year he has grown distant. He comes home exhausted from work and in most of our conversations he is barely present. Why is this happening and what can I do to regain the closeness?

Every couple begins their marriage "in love." And while they never set out to allow that love to fade, it often does—at least that "loving feeling" of intimacy fades. The couple may maintain a strong sense of commitment and even enjoy passionate relations, but their connectedness, their soul-mate quality, can easily slip into the background.

One of the most common reasons couples lose their intimacy is because they are running on a personal deficit. It's hard to be intimate, giving, and loving when you are busy, frazzled, and pressured. That's why each of you should spend some time on activities that restore your soul and your body. By giving yourselves some attention first (whether it be rest, exercise, reading, etc.), you store up energy you can use in your relationship.

When a couple experiences a crisis (loss of a job, financial debt, physical illness, loss of a loved one, etc.), it generally has one of two results. It either brings husband and wife closer together or drives them farther apart. Couples who face a crisis together, as a team, pool their resources and emerge from their crises stronger and more intimate. Those who allow a crisis to fracture their unity naturally lose their sense of intimacy.

Another reason some couples lose that loving feeling is that they become bored. They get stuck in a rut: five days of working, coming home, eating the same foods in the same atmosphere, waiting for the weekend that ends up being just like the others. After a while, the comfort that such a routine pattern provides begins to lose its luster and the couple's intimacy does too. Some couples are so entrenched in their day-in, day-out lives that they ever so gently ease into a dull marriage without intimacy and wake up one morning wondering what happened.

A final reason some couples lose their sense of intimacy sounds so obvious that it is embarrassing to mention: They don't work at it. This reason, however, is worth mentioning because so many couples simply expect intimacy to naturally be a part of their married lives. They expect intimacy to be automatic because they are husband and wife. But it doesn't work that way. Intimacy is something that needs to be cultivated, nurtured, and grown. Intimacy, like anything else worth having, requires work. When couples neglect this simple fact, their intimacy plummets.

So if you and your husband are going to regain the closeness you once had (and we definitely believe you can), you are going to need to rejuvenate your own spirits, get out of your rut by trying new things together, and face up to the fact that intimacy requires work. You won't always have a ten out of ten on the intimacy scale. It's not meant to be at full throttle all of the time. But you can maintain a higher level of intimacy than you currently have in your marriage if you accept the fact that intimacy doesn't happen naturally.

I understand that intimacy takes work, and I am willing to work at it. But what kind of specific advice can you offer on how to keep romance alive in our marriage?

Our friend Norm Wright has said, "What is romantically special to one couple may not be so to another."[4] We couldn't agree more. And when it comes to answering the question of how to keep romance alive, we want to preface it by saying that these suggestions are guidelines to help you carve your own path to keeping romance alive. Only you will know for sure what really works for your unique relationship.

To get you started, however, see the "Marital Intimacy Checkup" designed by Howard and Charlotte Clinebell on the next page.[5] Take a moment to discuss each of the areas and then check the blanks that apply to your relationship.

Taking time to complete the Marital Intimacy Checkup will help you pinpoint some of the specific areas where you are especially vulnerable to losing out on some intimacy. Be sure to keep your vulnerable spots in mind as you study the following list of ways to keep romance alive:

1. *Work at personal improvement.* Every once in a while we will hear a spouse complain, "She isn't the person I married!" And we always think, of course not! Who would want to marry someone who is going to remain exactly the same? Personal growth and change are part of a healthy life. So what are you doing to become a better person? What are you doing, not just to improve your marriage, but to improve you? As you work at your own personal growth you will, by default, be helping your marriage grow. And positive growth always keeps romance alive.

2. *Spice up the ordinary.* Guard your relationship against boredom by not allowing yourselves and your relationship to fall into humdrum patterns. You can avoid this in a thousand ways. When you are driving together, for example, take a new route home. Try a new restaurant or cook a new entree. Avoid doing the same things each weekend by planning different activities you can look forward to. Boredom will steal your romance, but you can prevent it from even coming near your marriage by spicing up the ordinary activities of your daily lives.

3. *Share an activity you both enjoy.* One of the complaints we often hear from couples we counsel, especially the husbands, is

Marital Intimacy Checkup

	Wife Desires Improvement	Husband Desires Improvement	Both Desire Improvement	Both Husband & Wife Satisfied
1. *Sexual Intimacy*				
2. *Emotional Intimacy* (Being tuned to each other's wavelength)				
3. *Intellectual Intimacy* (Closeness in the world of ideas)				
4. *Aesthetic Intimacy* (Sharing in acts of creating beauty)				
5. *Creative Intimacy* (Sharing in acts of creating)				
6. *Recreational Intimacy* (Relating in experiences of fun and play)				
7. *Work Intimacy* (Closeness of sharing common tasks)				
8. *Crisis Intimacy* (Closeness in coping with problems and pain)				
9. *Conflict Intimacy* (Facing and struggling with differences)				

that they don't have an activity they can do that is equally enjoyable. In other words, he might play basketball once a week with a buddy from work and she might garden with a friend, but they don't have an activity they do as husband and wife. Actually this can be quite difficult for some couples. If you are one of them, work at it. Have a brainstorming session together by making a list of possible activities (doing puzzles, hiking in the mountains, collecting rare books, etc.). Then rate them individually and compare your ratings. Next, try them out. By finding an activity to share, you will have an important tool for keeping the romantic soul-mate quality of your marriage alive and well.

4. *Focus on being a team.* Sometimes it is easy to pursue one's own goals, professionally and personally, while neglecting the goals you have as a couple. You can keep this from happening by remembering to function as a team. Consult each other as much as possible. For example, don't assume your partner isn't interested in a decision you have to make tomorrow at work. Ask him how he might handle it. Bring your partner into your life as much as you can and as your partner does the same, the two of you will forge a bond that will sustain romance over the life span of your marriage. As Antoine De Saint-Exupéry said, "Love does not consist in gazing at each other but in looking together in the same direction."

5. *Be quiet before God together.* This is perhaps the most neglected, yet most effective, way of keeping intimacy and romance alive in marriage. You might not think so, but spending quiet moments together reading and talking about spiritual matters, listening to God together, really does improve a couple's romance. As strange as it may sound, prayer even heightens sexual intimacy. Couples who pray together have more sex![6] Sharing a worship experience at church is also a great way of spending time before God together. We know a couple who has regular

spiritual retreats—just the two of them, alone with God. You can bet their romance is alive and well.

My husband doesn't ever touch me unless he wants sex. I enjoy our passionate times together, but I would also love for him to touch me at other times too. What can I do?

It sounds like your husband feels pretty strongly about not touching except in the heat of passion. As a man, I (Les) can identify with him to some degree. I have never been a "touchy-feely" kind of guy myself. Earlier in our marriage, I had no idea how much this hurt Leslie. Over the years I have softened, and the benefits are countless.

In her book *Anatomy of Love*, anthropologist Helen Fisher describes the importance of touching in general: "Human skin is like a field of grass, each blade a nerve ending so sensitive that the slightest graze can etch into the human brain a memory of the moment."[7] You can pretty much draw your own conclusions from that image!

Physical touch is critical to building romance and intimacy in your marriage. And we don't just mean touch as it relates to sexual play. We are talking about a tender touch while your partner is doing almost any ordinary task. A gentle squeeze on your partner's shoulder as she is preparing a meal, or a soft rub on his back as he is reading a book, can communicate loving messages in ways our words never could. There is simply no more eloquent way to say "You are not alone," "I appreciate you," "I'm sorry," or "I love you" than through touch.

Because physical touch is so important to building an intimate marriage, we often suggest that couples talk about it. We suggest that they explore how touch was used in the home they grew up in. You might want to do the same. This simple exercise can give a much better understanding of how and why the two of you may have different "touch quotients."

You might also explore how each of you likes to be touched and how you don't like to be touched. Maybe paying the bills makes you uptight and you want to have your space during that time. Let your partner know that isn't a good time for a gentle back rub. Or maybe because paying the bills makes you uptight it is an especially good time for a nice caress. You get the point. Make your wishes known. Take the guesswork out of communicating through physical touch.

My husband can be a big baby when he gets sick. I'm just the opposite when I get ill; I hate to admit I need help. Both of us annoy the other with our differing coping styles, but we want to deal with these times better. What's your advice?

Most couples don't pay too much attention to the phrase in their wedding vows that says "in sickness and in health." But sooner or later reality hits. Everybody gets sick—a sprained ankle, migraine headache, allergies, upset stomach, pneumonia, or the common cold—and knowing how to cope and care for a sick spouse can be tricky business.

Few things are more frustrating than seeing your husband or wife suffer and knowing that there is next to nothing you can do to end the suffering. However, there are some things you can do to manage your marriage more effectively during this difficult time. If you find your spouse battling an illness, consider the following suggestions:

First, learn as much as you can about the illness. What causes it? What's the prognosis? Can medication help? If so, what are the side effects? Talk to your doctor to learn what you can do to help the healing process. Don't be shy. If you have questions, speak up and use the phone when necessary. Gaining information eases anxiety and takes a lot of the stress out of being sick.

Second, learn as much as you can about your partner's idiosyncrasies when he or she is sick. Do you have special requests when you are flat on your back feeling miserable—a certain kind of food or beverage, the lights a certain way, the covers just so? Be sensitive to your partner's special requests and do your best to fulfill them if it helps the healing process. If they want a certain kind of cracker you normally don't buy, then buy it. Generally speaking, the better you meet your partner's needs, the quicker he or she will get well.

Third, balance your honest communication of frustrations with genuine support and encouragement. There is nothing wrong with using an appropriate time to tell your partner how you are feeling ("It's hard for me to go to work when you are feeling this way") as long as you also let him or her know how much you care ("I want to do anything I can to help you get better"). One of the best ways to do this, by the way, is through touch. Hold your partner's hand when you can. Touch is powerful medicine.

Fourth, pray for a healthy recovery. Ask God to give you wisdom in helping you deal with your partner's illness. Ask God to adjust your attitude, if necessary. Once you have prayed on your own, pray with your spouse. God will help you care for each other as you honor your marriage vows in sickness and in health!

What are some of the most helpful resources on intimacy in marriage?

Holding On to Romance by H. Norman Wright (Regal, 1992).

> In this book, marriage expert Norman Wright shows couples how to recapture the elusive feeling of romance and intimacy. He points to the fact that your spouse cannot know you unless you invite him or her into your inner world. But he doesn't just leave you there. He shows you how to cultivate intimacy by speaking your spouse's language and pros-

pering in the midst of a "love recession." The bottom line is that this book walks you through specific things you can do and say to rekindle the passion that first drew you together.

The Intimacy Factor by David and Jan Stoop (Thomas Nelson, 1993).

The Stoops demonstrate how family history, early behavior, birth order, and general home environment all contribute in a profound and critical way to shaping your personality and the way you relate to your spouse. Once you understand these influences, and your different personality types, you will be able to build a more intimate relationship with your spouse. According to the Stoops, "Intimacy is not a goal in and of itself. It is much like happiness: The more you actively seek it, the more elusive it becomes. Intimacy is a by-product of the right kinds of behaviors."

Intimate Marriage by Charles M. Sell (Multnomah, 1982).

"This book is designed to help the two of you make the most important discovery of all—each other." So writes the author of this helpful book. He points out that individual differences can work for marriage intimacy, not against it. Covering everything from sensuality to conflict, Charles Sell shows you how to cultivate intimacy even when it seems impossible. This is a book built on the conviction that in spite of negative emotions and differences of opinion, spiritual, emotional, and physical oneness in marriage *is* achievable.

CHAPTER EIGHT:
QUESTIONS ABOUT MONEY

My wife and I came from homes where money was handled differently. In my home Dad always paid the bills, but in my wife's home both her mom and dad shared financial matters more. How do we decide who should pay the bills and balance the checking account?

Few dimensions of married life are as important, yet as difficult, as the management of financial resources. Financial matters have long been one of the most widely reported causes of family discord, and almost eighty percent of young couples who divorce by age thirty report that financial problems were a primary cause of the divorce.[1] It is therefore imperative that you know "who should do what" when it comes to money.

Whether you and your partner have lots of or little cash to spare, it's always a good idea for partners to share equally the responsibilities of budgeting, investing, and saving money. When you're dividing up tasks, consider your talents and interests rather than assume stereotypical roles. Who gets a bigger paycheck doesn't determine who is more of a financial whiz or the better accountant. Similarly, some debts may be more emotionally stressful for one partner than for the other. Alimony payments, money owed to family members, doctors' bills—if there's a negative connection for one partner, maybe the other could handle writing the checks. The point is to take as much of the stress out of money in your marriage as possible.

To help you determine the roles each of you will play in your marriage money matters, here is a chart for you to complete:

	Husband	*Wife*	*Both*
Paying the bills	___	___	___
Balancing the checkbook	___	___	___
Tracking investments	___	___	___
Tracking expenses	___	___	___
Setting up a budget	___	___	___
Making big purchases	___	___	___

Once you complete this brief exercise, take time to talk about your agreed-upon roles. Why is each of you doing certain things? Why are you doing some things together? The point is to talk about money issues. If you do, you will be a step ahead of most couples who somehow expect money matters to fall naturally into place and then end up wondering why they don't like the way it turned out. '

I have some friends who have been married several years, and they each have their own checking account. They think we should do the same, but something about that doesn't feel right. What do you think? Is it a good idea for couples to have separate bank accounts?

In many marriages, stress builds up around money because of a "yours and/or mine" attitude. The stickiest issue, in fact, for two-income couples, especially in the early years of marriage, is choosing between separate and joint bank accounts.

The question of whether money should be pooled seems to have no right answer. Some researchers have found that couples who favored pooling their money were neither more nor less satisfied with their money management than couples who insisted on keeping their money separate. Nevertheless, both types of couples felt that their system was the right way to handle money.[2]

Pooling both incomes is usually the simplest way to go. It requires fewer accounts to balance, for one thing. Also, each spouse knows what the other spouse is doing monetarily. On the other hand, pooling can lead to confusion and being overdrawn at the bank if partners are writing checks unknown to the other. The solution to this, of course, is to keep each other informed and up-to-date on expenses.

Whether you hold joint or separate accounts or have one income or two, be sure you take great pains to make buying decisions as equal as possible. It's also a good idea to set aside a monthly amount of personal spending money for each of you. There's a definite psychological benefit to having your own private bit of money to do with as you wish, no matter how small the sum.

Neither of us is a financial wizard. In fact, money isn't a high priority for us. However, we both know that we need to have a way of managing our income and expenses in a way that fits our style. How do we start a budget and stick to it?

Mention "budget" to some people and they immediately bristle. "Why get an ulcer worrying about nickels and dimes," they think to themselves. "I don't like to be tied down to numbers."

If you fit into that category, take a deep breath. Budgets aren't as bad as you might think. In fact, the real goal of a good budget is to give you more freedom. It is a plan of spending to assure that you get whatever it is you need and want.

The truth is, we all budget informally. If you want to buy a new wardrobe but do not have the money to do so and choose not to buy it on credit, then you are budgeting. To budget formally, however, is to deliberately gain better control over all of your financial life—so it doesn't control you.

You can think of budgeting very simply as allotting money for necessities and then divvying up money that is left over for other wants. How does this save you money? Consider shopping at the grocery. It is estimated that the spontaneous food shopper spends approximately fifteen percent more for food than the shopper who has a planned food budget and a shopping list of needed items. Without a specific limit, it is extremely easy to buy impulsively.

You can create a budget by following these four basic steps:

1. Analyze past spending by keeping careful records for a month or two of everything you spend.
2. Determine fixed expenses such as rent and any other contractual payments that must be made (even if they are infrequent, such as insurance and taxes).
3. Determine flexible expenses, such as food, clothing, and entertainment.
4. Balance your fixed plus flexible expenditures with your available income. If a surplus exists, you can apply it toward achieving your goals of buying a home or other investments. If there is a deficit, reexamine your flexible expenditures. You can also reexamine fixed expenses with a view to reducing them in the future (by changing your standard of living).

The following is a sample monthly budget that may help you get a better idea of how to structure your budget:

Fixed Expenses	Estimate	Actual
Rent	425	425
Electricity	28	28
Insurance	16	16
Loan or other debt	55	55
Savings	50	50

Giving	165	165
Total Fixed Expenses	**739**	**739**
Flexible Expenses		
Food	250	228
Clothing	100	164
Fuel	25	22
Phone	20	18
Entertainment	150	120
Total Flexible Expenses	**545**	**552**
Net Monthly Income	1,450	1,450
Total Monthly Expense	-1,284	-1,291
Balance	**166**	**159**

In this particular budget, the couple decided to make savings and giving a part of their fixed payments (not a bad idea!). Their flexible expenses are fairly minimal. After subtracting all expenses from their income they have a surplus of $166 that they may use to supplement their expenses or to contribute to their savings. Setting up a budget is really pretty simple—the trick is sticking with it.

The only way to make sure you are carrying out your budget is by keeping records of what you are actually spending. The ultimate way to maintain records is to write everything down. This can be accomplished by simply taking a moment to put it in a datebook or on a piece of scrap paper and then tally up your expenses every so often throughout the month to see where you stand. In the sample budget, you can see that the couple spent more on clothing than they budgeted, but since other expenses were not as much and since they had a little buffer in their balance, it did not affect them too much.

A couple thoughts to remember: The key to managing your money is keeping track of where it is going. Also, it is important to remember that budgets are used for a specified time and then updated to reflect changing circumstances. As dull and uninteresting as budget planning may seem, the couple that does not put time into planning and controlling their finances may face increasing monetary strain and eventually end up with their finances controlling them.

Still not convinced that a budget is for you? You may be right. The truth is, budgets are not the answer for every couple. They sometimes become just another way to fail on a monthly basis. However, we recommend that you try budgeting at least short-term. See how it works for you. Reevaluate after a few months and tinker with your plan until both of you are happy.

We want to save money for our future and we try to keep our hands off a portion of the money in our checking account, but it's not working. Each month we seem to dip into whatever we wanted to set aside. There has to be a better way. What's your advice on the best way to save money for the future?

Most young people are baffled by how to reach their long-term financial goals such as paying for their children's education, buying a house, or planning for retirement. The best way to achieve these objectives is to accumulate faithfully over time—experts suggest ten to fifteen percent but even small percentages add up—and to invest the money to insure that funds are preserved until you need them.

It is no secret that the sooner you get started, the greater your return will be. For example, if you invest $1,000 annually at five percent interest, you will have $5,525 in five years. But in forty years you'll have $120,800. It all has to do with compound interest, or "interest on interest." That is, if the interest (earned on an investment) is itself reinvested, this investment of interest will itself earn interest.

Think of it this way. Suppose you could invest $100 per month at ten percent compound interest. Then, after seven years, suppose you began to withdraw $100 per month (making no further deposits). How long could you continue such withdrawals before exhausting the principal? Eight years? Sixteen years? Twenty-four years? The answer is forever. This is because in seven years you would be earning $100 a month on your money. You could withdraw $100 each month forever, leaving the principal untouched, as long as you were still earning ten percent in interest.

A good investment balances three factors: safety, yield, and growth. If an investment is safe but provides a yield less than the rate of inflation and no growth at all, it is obviously a poor investment. If the investment provides safety and a relatively high yield but fails to grow with the economy, it is also a poor investment. Finally, if growth is phenomenal and yield outstanding but the risks are great, it's obviously a poor investment; in fact, this is properly called "speculating" rather than investing.

One classic investment is bonds, which pay a fixed rate over their lifetime. The drawback to bonds, however, is that this fixed rate might look good at the time of purchase but may not be adequate in a time of rapid inflation. Stocks are another traditional investment vehicle. Since they are unpredictable, however, experts advise that no more than five percent of one's investment funds should be put into any single stock.[3] Also, since it is difficult for the nonprofessional to keep track of a great number of stocks, one solution is buying shares in a mutual fund (rather than an individual stock). A mutual fund is an investment company that pays a professional money manager to buy stocks in anticipation of their rising value and sell them when they appear to be near their peak value. When you buy a share in a mutual fund, you buy a share in the entire portfolio of stocks the fund owns.

When it comes to making a sound investment, beware of get-rich-quick schemes and remember the three cardinal principles of investing: safety, yield, and growth—with safety of paramount importance. Finally, begin your investment program as early as possible to take advantage of the growth-on-growth feature of compound interest, invest regularly, be patient, and seek the help of a trusted money manager who can give you sound advice for your particular situation. As Proverbs says: "The wise man saves for the future, but the foolish man spends whatever he gets" (21:20 TLB).

We hate to admit it, but we started our marriage in significant financial debt. We spent more than we should have on our wedding and honeymoon, and then we both had pretty big school bills. We hate the financial burden we are under and want to get out of debt. How do we do it?

Too many couples are drowning in debt. Each year, the average couple spends four hundred dollars more than they earn, and twenty-three percent of the average American's take-home pay is already committed to pay existing debt, not including the home mortgage!

The huge amounts of debt most couples carry should probably come as no surprise since the gospel according to Madison Avenue is buy now and pay later. So couples take bank loans, borrow money from relatives, have past-due medical bills, and of course use the power of the plastic credit card. The problem with Madison Avenue's philosophy is that the debt of temporary freedom eventually puts us in financial prison. That's why Scripture speaks so directly about debt: "The rich rule over the poor, and the borrower is servant to the lender" (Proverbs 22:7). The apostle Paul puts it this way: "You were bought at a price; do not become slaves of men" (1 Corinthians 7:23). By legally obligating ourselves to meet our debts, we lose the freedom of deciding where to spend our income. Most financial experts agree that the only three reasons to go into debt are to buy a home, to finance a business, or to pay for an education.

So what do you do if you are carrying debt that is not healthy? We recommend starting with a written budget to help you analyze your spending pattern, plan ahead, and curb your impulsive spending. Next, determine whether there is anything you do not really need that might be sold to enable you to get out of debt more quickly. Are you living beyond your means by having a certain car, for example? The next step is to make a comprehensive list of everything you owe and the interest rate your creditors are charging for each debt. You will want to pay off those charging the highest rate of interest first. This will lead you to establish a debt repayment schedule for each creditor by noting the monthly payment, the months remaining, and the balance due. Put this in writing so you know exactly where you stand and where you have to go.

The next step may be to consider earning additional income. Earning a little additional income, even temporarily, may be a solution if you can do so without harming your marriage. Next, take special care not to accumulate new debt. This can be done through the proverbial "plastic surgery" of cutting up your credit cards. The little cards are dangerous. It has been shown that people spend approximately one-third more when they use credit cards rather than cash, probably because they feel they are not really spending money. Pay for things with cash or check. Along these same lines, delay your gratification and be content with what you have. If you persevere you will eventually become debt free. It is hard work to get there, but there is no magic involved, no special tricks—just discipline and perseverance. So don't give up. The freedom to be gained is worth the effort.

Once you have gotten out of debt, you can avoid getting back into it by saving in an interest-bearing account for major purchases. Over the years, we all face major purchases such as buying an automobile, appliances, or furniture. Prepare ahead by setting aside money for big-ticket items. You will then be able to pay cash for items that most people buy on credit. You can even do this when buying an automobile (though only thirty percent of couples do). The average person keeps a car between three and four years. The average car lasts ten years. Here is how to escape using credit: First, decide in advance to keep your car for at least six years; second, pay off your automobile loan; third, continue paying the monthly car payment to yourself in a special savings account. Then when you are ready to replace your car, the savings plus the trade-in should be sufficient to buy the next car without credit. With a little planning and a lot of discipline, you can live debt free and enjoy countless benefits as a result.

My wife likes to spend money; I want to save for a house. She will buy something without even knowing the price while I count every cent as we go through the grocery aisles. Compromising on how we spend money has been our number-one source of conflict in marriage. What do we do when one of us is a spender and the other is a hoarder?

It is not uncommon for one person in a couple to be a live-for-today spender and the other to be a compulsive saver. It seems these styles emerge to some degree or another in nearly every marriage. And while these money styles can be exasperating, it *is* possible to work the bugs out when the styles clash.

We did. When we first got married, I (Leslie) had no concept of saving money for the future while Les, from my perspective, was fanatical about it. He can delay his gratification like no one else I know, and this created a lot of friction. However, after more than a dozen years of marriage, we have found a comfortable balance where both of us feel respected and our unique needs are met. Maybe what worked for us will help you.

Start by discussing your spending styles with each other. How did your childhoods shape your beliefs about money? How were financial decisions made? Were money problems discussed openly? What are your spending priorities? Are they in sync with your partner's? Don't be disturbed if you find that your priorities conflict. The goal is to communicate and compromise, not to evaluate and judge. If you let go of right or wrong, it will be a lot easier to give and take.

Above all, show respect. Recognize that it's possible to admire your husband's cavalier attitude toward spending money or your wife's knack for saving it. Remember, no right or wrong, just differences. Try putting yourselves in each other's shoes to see things from the opposite perspective. A little empathy can go a long way toward creating compromise.

If you find that you are developing a pattern of having the same disagreements over money again and again, the true source of dissension may not be your money styles. That's when it's time to look for the real agenda of your arguments. For example, if the hidden agenda is a question of power, you may find yourself saying, "You must think I'm too dumb to understand our finances!" Or you might resort to personal attacks: "You always have to be the boss and make every single decision yourself."

When intense money battles erupt between you, it is always good to ask yourself: "Are we still talking about money, or is the real issue something else entirely?" Another important tip is to not work through money problems while one of you is angry. Instead, schedule some time when you are both a little calmer. Finally, if you still find yourself in a stalemate over a money issue—fighting more and compromising less—then consider consulting an objective third party who is trained in dealing with financial and communication issues. Talk to your pastor or a trusted counselor for a good referral. Getting this issue resolved is worth the effort. It just might save your marriage.

What are the best resources on money and marriage?

The Christian's Guide to Worry-free Money Management by Daniel B. Busby, Kent E. Barber, and Robert L. Temple (Zondervan, 1994).

When it comes to money, the Bible has a lot to say, and it makes it very clear that God expects us to be stewards of the resources entrusted to us. *The Christian's Guide to Worry-free Money Management* explains in a step-by-step fashion how to apply principles of responsible stewardship in your personal finances. It provides a money management system that fulfills God's commandments and frees you from financial worries. Study questions, practical tips, and worksheets in this resource will help you plot a path toward financial security.

The Christian's Guide to Wise Investing by Gary D. Moore (Zondervan, 1990, 1994).

Whether you have $500 or $50,000 to invest, *The Christian's Guide to Wise Investing* gives you the knowledge you need to be smart with your money. If you have ever experienced confusion from experts' exotic talk about the myriad of financial investment options, rest assured you will not find that in this volume. It is written with a firm footing in biblical principles and in clear, concise language you will understand.

Secrets to Financial Success in Marriage by John C. Shimer (Successful Financial Planners, 1993).

Far more than just a manual on banking and budgeting, this book gives couples a larger picture of the importance of money in marriage. It examines such diverse topics as how to talk about dreams and make them come true, the relationship between personal values and money, and so on. This book is not about getting rich. Instead, it is about building a happy, prosperous, and balanced partnership.

CHAPTER NINE:
QUESTIONS ABOUT OTHER RELATIONSHIPS

When we were in college together, we had a lot of the same friends. But since moving away, we don't have a "gang" of friends we hang out with. In fact, we don't have very many mutual friends at all, and that troubles me. Should it? I mean, should married couples have separate sets of friends?

We recently counseled a couple who had suffered a meltdown. Their marriage was falling apart after just three years, and they came to see us as a last-ditch effort. Actually, they came to see us after the husband had already decided it was over. As they unraveled their story, we learned that most of their dating relationship was done long distance, with him living in Seattle and her in Phoenix. When they got married, she left her job in Phoenix to join him. A problem arose, however, when she realized he had no intention of including her in his circle of friends. He maintained his social network and she was left, more or less, to fend for herself. She made a few friends at her new job, but felt terribly rejected by her husband.

There were plenty of other factors contributing to their breakup (like the husband's lack of empathy for his wife), but their separate social circles created a huge chasm between them.

Is the moral of this case that you shouldn't have separate friends as husband and wife? No. But it does indicate that we need to be thoughtful about how our social network impacts our marriage. Here are a few suggestions:

1. *Keep each other informed.* Even if your friends' paths don't cross with your partner's, there is no reason to keep either one in the dark. Let your spouse know about your friends: what they are like, what you talk about, and so on. It's also a good idea to let your friends know about your spouse. Even if they never meet, they will feel that they know one another, and it keeps your world of separate friends from being foreign or mysterious.

2. *Include your spouse in activities with your friends when possible.* If you have a friend at work, for example, and you rarely see each other out of that context, you might invite him or her to your home for a meal and to meet your spouse. If nothing else, you might have your spouse informally drop by the office to at least associate a name with a face. This allows your partner to have a much better idea of who you are talking about when you mention your friend at work.

3. *Work to initiate shared friendships that balance out your social network.* If you find that many of your friends are in a separate circle from your spouse, you will need to make a conscious effort to cultivate and maintain friendships that you both share. Talk about it together to find out how each of you is feeling about your circle of friends. If the scales need to be tipped, work on it by taking some initiative to build friendships you can have in common.

My husband has a woman friend at work with whom he spends a lot of time, and I recently read a magazine article called "When Friends Become Lovers." I can't help feeling jealous. Should I be worried? Can men and women be just friends?

Your concern is understandable. We don't know of any couple who, at one time or another, hasn't been a little nervous about each other having opposite-sex friends. Some couples tell us it's okay with them in theory, but they always want to know every word of conversation between their spouse and the friend. Other couples are downright against it, believing that it's always risky business. In fact, we recently spoke at a very large church in Florida where Sunday school classes for all ages are segregated into male and female groups.

In his helpful book *Can Men and Women Be Just Friends?*, Andy Bustanoby includes a "Couples' Friendship Inventory" for evaluating opposite-sex relationships involving married couples. Here is a sampling of the items. See how many you agree with:

- You worry about how much he/she sees this other person.
- You feel that this other person is more important than you.
- You're afraid to upset him/her because it may result in his/her seeking comfort from this other person.
- You find yourself spying on him/her to confirm your suspicions about this relationship.
- You sometimes feel guilty over the ways you have tried to intervene in this relationship.

Bustanoby includes fourteen items in all and says that if you agree with three or more of them that you may have very understandable reasons for raising suspicions.

Regardless of how you feel about the friendship your husband has with the woman at work, we do believe it is possible for men and women to be just friends—as long as they understand that the friendship is about something besides each other. If the friendship, for example, results from a shoulder-to-shoulder effort where the focus is on a common interest rather than on each other, a level of mutual appreciation will naturally develop and can be quite healthy. However, if the friendship becomes an insiders' club where "nobody else understands us," red flags go up for us.

A healthy opposite-sex friendship is transparent and out in the open. It doesn't have an appearance of secretiveness or privacy. There is a wholesome inclusion of others—and that includes spouses.

I have always had lots of guy friends. As a woman, I can relate just as well, if not easier, to men. I know it bothers my husband and I don't want him to feel uneasy about this, but I also don't want to sever all ties with my opposite-sex friends. What should I do?

You are very wise to take your husband's feelings into consideration on this matter. It says that you care deeply about him and your relationship. But your strong desire to maintain relationships that may trouble him urges us to ask you a question: Which relationship is more important to you, the relationships with your male friends or the relationship with your husband?

Assuming you answered that your husband was most important to you, we offer a few suggestions on how to enjoy your friendships with other men while at the same time making it very clear that you prize, above all other relationships, the one you have with your husband.

For starters, don't trust yourself. Sexual feelings are, in great part, biological, and at times sexual desire can rush in when we aren't prepared for it. Never assume you (or any of your friends) are in complete control of these feelings—especially if you and your husband are not getting along well.

Second, stay clear of friendships where the other man is in a weak marriage and is hungry for love. You may have compassion for his suffering, but the chemistry makes boundary issues too precarious.

Third, think through the setting in which you meet. This is important. Some settings are more sexual than others, and you need to stay clear of them. Just the two of you at a candlelight dinner, for example, is not a good idea under any circumstances. Be sensible about settings.

Fourth, fill your spouse in every time you meet with your opposite-sex friend. Keep him informed of where you went and what you talked about. If you find yourself being protective or secretive, that is a danger sign.

Fifth, never allow any form of physical contact to take place in a private setting. If and when you show affection, do it in front of others.

Finally, draw the line if you need to. If you feel that the relationship has potential to become something much more than a friendship, remember how precious your marriage is to you and set strict boundaries on the friendship (e.g., that you will be together only when your spouse is also present).

These guidelines are simple and based on common sense. But when an opposite-sex friendship loses control, the supply of common sense suddenly becomes very low.

There is a guy at work who often flirts with me (as well as other women workers). I have no feelings for him in the least, but I don't want to tell my husband about it because I'm afraid he might take it the wrong way and get upset. What should I do?

Flirting, that amorous play and coquettish behavior that traditionally begins a dating relationship, can be downright disconcerting when it is exhibited anywhere else. When somebody flirts with you or your spouse, even innocently, it's a threat, not a compliment.

Everyone knows it now: What some men consider innocent flirtations most women consider harassment. Women, of course, have felt this all along, but now we know it for fact. According to a recent study at Bucknell University, flirting for men is a more serious activity. There's more ego at stake. It becomes sort of a conquest. For women, on the other hand, it's more of a playful activity. It's an end, rather than a means to an end.

Whether you should tell your husband about this guy depends a lot on how aggressive this fellow is. If your spouse were to get unduly anxious about a seemingly innocent incident, it may be better to keep it to yourself. But if this guy is really beginning to creep you out, it's probably best to talk to your husband about him. Either way, there are several things you can do to cope effectively with the predicament.

First, you need to have a ready comeback for the next time this guy flirts with you. There is a line that can do wonders in most situations. It is: "Hold on for a minute. As two professionals, let's talk about what just happened." A statement like this doesn't require you to get huffy or preachy. But it immediately cools off the person's ardor and puts you in charge. It brings whatever just happened to a rational and professional level. On top of that, the person will be surprised at how composed and together you are. This statement will startle him into realizing you have no intentions of anything but a completely professional work situation. Simply saying, "Hold on for a minute. Let's talk about this as two professional colleagues," allows you to reestablish the camaraderie that you will need in order to get this person to treat you as an equal.

Next, you need to take every precaution not to flirt back. Perhaps you are thinking, "What's the big deal with a little flirtatious fun?" Maybe you believe there is little harm in flirting back with your pursuer. If you do, you are playing with fire. All flirting is sexual and creates an immediate aura of arousal between two consenting people. This is one of the chief pleasures of flirting. Indeed, biologists have recently discovered that the chemistry between a flirting couple is more than a metaphor. Flirting triggers a series of hormonal and neural changes that typically accompany pleasurable sexual activities. So face the fact that you are flirting with disaster.

Finally, you need to realize that as a married person you have at your disposal one of the most effective techniques for diffusing coquettish behavior. Whether at work, at church, or anywhere else, this technique is one of your best bets for putting water on a flirt's fire. Simply make a point of showing affection for your partner. If he or she is present, hold hands. If you are alone, talk about him and keep talking about him. You can flirt-proof your office by displaying plenty of pictures of your mate, too. Openly expressing affection for your spouse shows the flirt that you are not interested in anyone else. One more thing along these lines: Be careful not to tease or criticize your mate in front of others. This can be lethal in front of a flirt. He or she will read it as a sign that you're not happy with your mate and take it as encouragement to flirt.

Talking to your husband about this situation at work can help you strategize more ways of combating this flirtatious behavior, and it can also reinforce your faithfulness to your husband. By talking to him about it, he will know that you are fully committed and are wanting to do everything possible to protect your marriage.

My husband has never met my boss, but from the stories I tell him, he thinks that my boss may be sexually harassing women at work. How do I know if I am the victim of sexual harassment, and what should I do if I am?

Prior to the middle seventies, sexual harassment probably was common but nobody used the term. People didn't know what to call overly flirtatious behavior and sexual aggression that belittled women. Once sexual harassment had a name, however, organizations attempted to define more specifically what it involved. One of the most common definitions appeared in the

Journal of Social Problems: "Behavior that includes verbal sexual suggestions or jokes; constant leering or ogling; 'accidental' brushing against a woman's body; a 'friendly' pat, squeeze, or arm around her; catching her alone for a quick kiss; the explicit proposition backed by threat of losing her job; and forced sexual relations." This kind of behavior is a blight on society and wrong in any situation.

Even if your boss's comments and actions are disguised as flattery, they may fall into the category of sexual harassment. If this is the case, he has not only violated your personal boundaries, he has broken the law. It is at this point that you have every right to file a complaint with the State Department of Fair Employment or with the Federal Equal Employment Opportunity Commission who will investigate your claim.

If your boss's behavior is not harassment, but you think it has the potential to be, do some preventative work. For example, don't allow yourself to be cornered. This can solve the problem with your boss before it even begins and save you (and your husband) a lot of emotional turmoil. If your internal radar is correct, the best thing you can do is stay clear. Don't allow yourself to be caught alone with him. Use any excuse—going to the rest room, for example—to avoid giving him or her the opportunity to make a pass.

Since realizing that so many of our friendships are independent of each other, we have decided to build relationships with other couples. However, that is a lot harder to do than we thought it would be. What can we do to build relationships with other couples?

You are right. It can be very tough to find another couple where both of you hit it off with the other two. In reality, you are actually building not just one relationship but four. That's a lot to pull off all at once. However, it is possible, and here are a few practical ways of building relationships with other couples.

1. *Plan outings or brief getaways.* Take some initiative to coordinate an activity or a weekend away with another couple. We recently took a trip with another couple we had lost touch with and quickly rekindled our friendship. A little initiative in this area can bring great results.

2. *Make a commitment to hospitality.* One of the best ways of meeting other couples and cultivating mutual friendships is by opening up your home. It doesn't have to be a special occasion to invite others over for a meal or even a dessert. Once people have been to your home, camaraderie is more likely to develop.

3. *Join a small couples group or Sunday school class.* Your local church can be one of the best places to get acquainted with other couples. A Sunday school class or small group for couples is ideal for finding fellowship. If your church doesn't have anything like this, start your own or look around for a church that does have one.

4. *Maintain contact.* One of the reasons many couples friendships don't work is that it simply takes effort to maintain them. If you find another couple you both enjoy, initiate contact and schedule time together.

5. *Be open to a variety of friendships.* Sometimes the couples you may not be thinking about can become good friends. For example, you might find that you have more in common with an older couple than you think. Be open to different kinds of friendships. It will enrich your social life.

After trying some of these tips you may still come up empty-handed. But don't give up. Like all good relationships, these friendships take time to emerge and develop.

Our church doesn't have a couples fellowship group and we'd like to be in one. We could go to another church, but we'd like to stay where we are. Do you have any ideas on how to start a couples fellowship group?

We have been in several groups together and find them very beneficial. In fact, we started one with three other couples in graduate school that met for five years.

You don't have to be a specialist in marriage or anything else to get a couples group going. In fact, it's quite simple. You can begin by identifying two to four other couples you would like to get to know better. These may be couples at your church or maybe from someplace else.

Next, make contact with each couple to see if they are interested and negotiate a possible meeting time and place. You may want to hold the first gathering at your home and then decide at that time where the group would like to meet. It often works well to meet at other group members' homes.

Another decision to be made by the group is how it will be structured. Will it meet weekly, biweekly, monthly, or what? And how long will each group time be?

Of course, a topic also needs to be discussed. Will the group study a book together, pray, play games, eat, or what? Some groups have the host couple for that meeting structure the evening.

These are just a few basic ideas to get you going. You can create any kind of group you desire. It simply takes initiative to get it going.

What are some of the most helpful resources on other relationships and marriage?

The Friendship Factor by Alan Loy McGinnis (Augsburg, 1979).

This best-selling book has become a classic on friendship. While it is not particularly for married couples, its principles certainly apply. Topics include "Five Ways to Deepen Your Relationships," "Five Guidelines for Cultivating Intimacy," "Two Ways to Handle Negative

Emotions Without Destroying the Relationship," and "What Happens When Your Relationships Go Bad?" The chapter titled "Eros: Its Power and Its Problems" is particularly helpful to married couples dealing with male-female friendships.

High-Maintenance Relationships: How to Handle Impossible People by Les Parrott III (Tyndale, 1996).

How do we cope with difficult relationships that affect our marriage? When should we love without limits, and when should we love with definite limits? *High-Maintenance Relationships* offers clear and direct answers for dealing with relationships that give so little but demand so much. Each chapter offers vignettes to help readers identify difficult relationships, a self-test to identify people who exemplify the high-maintenance relationship, and extensive coping strategies to deal with difficult people in several settings.

Can Men and Women Be Just Friends? by Andy Bustanoby (Zondervan, 1993).

In this book, Andy Bustanoby helps both men and women understand what friendship is, how to handle opposite-sex friendships, how to know when an outside "friendship" endangers your marriage, and how to make your spouse your best friend. In addition, the "Couples' Friendship Inventory" will help you evaluate the quality of the friendship in your marriage. This book gives clear, pointed advice on how to build strong, godly friendships

Chapter Ten:
Questions About Personality

My wife is so different from me. When we go to a party, she wants to float around and meet as many people as possible. I'd rather sit and talk with one or two people. She gets so frustrated with me. How can I make her understand that we are just different?

One of the most baffling tasks of married couples is to come to terms with fundamental personality differences between them.

How come my wife gives up so quickly when the pressure is on?

Why does he like to talk in abstract theoretical terms?

Why does she have to be so concrete and practical all the time?

How come he becomes so excitable and I'm more calm and collected?

Some couples spend years in needless frustration asking these kinds of questions because they falsely believe the only true resolution is to make their spouses think, feel, and behave more like them. That tactic, however, is doomed to failure. The key is to understand and appreciate one another's differences rather than change them.

One of the greatest steps you can take as a married couple is to begin the adventure of exploring your differing personality styles together. There are several ways of doing this. The traditional route is to pay a clinical psychologist to give you a battery of personality tests and then interpret the results. However, this can be a costly endeavor. Another way of achieving this goal is to acquire a few simple tools and set aside time together to assess your personality differences and then process the information.

One of the most accessible and helpful tools is contained in the book *Please Understand Me*. It is based on the idea (stemming from the theory of psychologist Carl Jung) that just as people are born with differing physical traits, so are we born with differing personality or temperament traits. In the 1950s Isabel Myers and Kathryn Briggs devised the Myers-Briggs Type Indicator test, a tool for identifying personality types based on various combinations of inborn temperament traits. *Please Understand Me* is an in-depth look at this concept, and it contains a self-test both of you can take and then interpret to discover some fundamental differences.

The self-test in *Please Understand Me* is built on four primary areas of difference: Extrovert/Introvert, Intuitive/Sensing, Thinking/Feeling, and Structured/Unstructured. These areas can form sixteen different combinations and in a matter of moments reveal significant ways in which you and your partner differ. You may both be fairly intuitive, but be polar opposites on the introvert/extrovert scale. Maybe one of you is a thinker and the other a feeler.

The goal of this process is not to simply discover differences and leave it at that, however. The goal is to allow your own talents and strengths to become the contributions you make to your marriage. This assessment tool is simply a means to doing everything possible to free one another to be who God made you to be. It won't take you long into this process to end up delighting in the very differences that once caused division. You see, once you discover one another's gifts and styles, each of you can take leadership in those areas where your abilities lie, not allowing predetermined gender roles to inhibit your marriage.

It's hard to appreciate, accept, and love someone authentically when you don't understand them. It's tough to resolve little conflicts when underlying personality traits are the real issue. Do yourself and your marriage a favor and avoid years of frustration by learning that the two of you are not better or worse than one another—just different. When you quit passing judgment on your differences, you will find fulfillment you never imagined possible in marriage.

Okay, so I understand that it is important to accept my husband's personality differences and not pass judgment on them, but how do I do it? How do I accept and appreciate our differences?

When it comes to personality differences, people are attracted to, and marry, their opposites with high frequency.[1] "Opposites attract," it turns out, is more than a cliché. People instinctively seek out their opposites. Something within us is fascinated by that which we aren't. We want to get closer to it, examine it, perhaps embrace it. But why, then, do so many couples become irritated and bothered by the opposite traits? The answer is that couples only get frustrated by opposites when they attempt to change each other.

We make a tremendous breakthrough once we recognize our impulse to instruct, criticize, or manipulate our spouse into being more like us. Be honest. We all do it. We think to ourselves: *If she would just do things the way I do, this would be a wonderful marriage.* The truth is it would be a terribly boring marriage! It is our differences that make marriage attractive, exciting, adventurous.

For that reason you must learn to resist the impulse to change one another. You must pause each time the impulse strikes, and button your lip—say nothing. Each time you suspend your audible evaluation and coercion (of trying to make your spouse be more spontaneous, more logical, more whatever), you take a step closer to accepting him or her as is. You move closer to appreciating what attracted you to your partner in the first place.

A simple pause is the first step in accepting one another's differences. A simple pause can lead you to empty yourself of your need to change one another. When both of you are practicing this emptying exercise, you will be amazed at how your marriage blooms. Rarely in life do two people intentionally give one another the grace to be who they are without judgment or critique.

So think about your partner's opposite traits. What is it about these traits that you find attractive? Sure, they may become irritating to you at times, but set that aside and focus on what you appreciate about these opposite traits. Maybe you are highly organized and efficient and your spouse is unencumbered by systems and neatness—and it drives you up the wall. *Why isn't she more like me?* you ask. Well, what would happen if she were like you? Wouldn't you miss her spontaneity and carefree spirit? Wouldn't you long for her happy-go-lucky attitude to return? You see, you cannot have your cake and eat it too in marriage. You cannot have your partner possess qualities that complement yours and still expect him or her to be just like you.

Once you accept this fact, you can relax in knowing that your partner's differences are what hold the potential to make your marriage more fulfilling.

I'm from a big family. In fact, I'm the firstborn in a family of six siblings. My wife is an only child. Will this affect our marriage, and if so, how?

This is an intriguing question, one that a lot of couples never think to ask. But it's important, just the same. Why? Because some experts who study family constellation believe that ignoring birth order can be bad for your marriage.

Pioneering psychologist Alfred Adler was the first to see a correlation between where a person was born into a family and that person's approach to life. He conducted extensive studies that showed that birth order is a significant factor in personality development, behavior, and outlook. Since that time, hundreds of psychologists have conducted research that confirmed his theory.

There are three major birth orders: firstborn, middle child, and last born (the only child usually takes on the characteristics of the firstborn). Dr. Kevin Leman, an expert in birth order and the author of *Were You Born for Each Other?*, has summarized the most salient characteristics (plus and minus) of each birth order in the following chart:[2]

	Plus	Minus
Firstborn	In control	Perfectionist
	Punctual	Moody
	Organized	Critical
	Conscientious	Stubborn
	Serious	Skeptical
	Scholastically minded	Tense
	Reliable	Driven
	Planner	Faultfinder
Middle Born	Intensely loyal	Feels inferior to others
	Good negotiator	Avoids confrontation
	Competitive	Feels squeezed and
	Well adjusted	closed in
	Social	Hides feelings
	Master of compromise	Easily embarrassed
	Peacemaker	
Last Born	Tolerant	Impulsive
	Personable	Irresponsible
	Sees others' point of view	Disorganized
	Easygoing	Manipulative
	Spontaneous	Self-centered
	Caring	Rebellious
	Affectionate	

When paired up in marriage, the nine combinations of birth order often reveal some helpful insights for many couples. When two firstborns marry, for example, a controller-pleaser pattern typically results. A firstborn and a last born, on the other hand, tend to develop a relationship in which the role of teacher-learner is more comfortable. A last born and a last born together in marriage are sure to have fun, but they may get out of control every once in a while.

The varying combinations of birth orders and their ramifications are too numerous to recount in detail here, but if this concept appeals to you and shows promise for insight into your marriage, we urge you to take a look at Kevin Leman's book.

My husband seems like a different person than the man I married, and I have a suspicion that he feels I have changed a lot too. Of course, neither of us feels that we changed, but something's different. What happened?

We know what you mean. During our fourth or fifth month of marriage each of us began wondering what had happened to the person we married. Doubts began to creep in quietly: "Did we make a mistake?" Both of us were feeling that the other person had changed in remarkable ways . . . and not for the better!

It took some time and a few months of therapy, but we eventually learned the truth. Neither of us had changed. Like almost every newlywed couple, we were simply beginning to see each other in a clearer light. We were changing our idealized picture of each other and seeing one another for who we really were. In fact, we were going one step further and exaggerating the differences between us: "If I didn't recognize this trait in him before we got married, what else have I missed?"

Bill and Lynne Hybels can attest to this same experience. He writes about it in his book *Honest to God?*:

> I dated Lynne off and on for five years, but it was not until after the wedding that I found out the awful truth. Lynne was

strange. She was not normal like me. To begin with, she turned out to be a near-recluse. . . . Then there was the issue of her oversensitivity. . . . She said I didn't care about people. Then there was the planning issue. She always had to have everything planned. . . . For years I believed that if I could just get her to be more like me, we could have a decent marriage. She thought the same about me. But God intervened. . . . [3]

Bill goes on to describe how taking the self-test in the book *Please Understand Me* helped turn their marriage around at just the point when they needed it. Each of them felt their partner's personality had changed after marriage. Of course, it hadn't; they just saw each other—as every couple who eventually gets married does—in a different light.

So if you are feeling that your partner's personality changed after you got married, it might be time to invest in an assessment of your temperaments. Learning the fundamental differences between you, the ones that existed before the two of you even met, can help ease a lot of anxiety and tension.

What are some of the most helpful resources on personality types and marriage?

Were You Born for Each Other? by Kevin Leman (Delacorte, 1991).

Birth order expert Dr. Kevin Leman applies his research to the marriage relationship in this book and claims that the secret to romantic happiness doesn't lie in chemistry, timing, or even luck. Leman believes very strongly in birth order, pointing to it as the most important factor in marriage. While we wouldn't go that far, we find many of his insights on personality in marriage to be helpful. He describes what each birth order—firstborn, middle born, and last born—is like within a marriage. Among other things, he deals with how to cope if your birth orders aren't ideally suited for one another.

Please Understand Me: Character & Temperament Types by David Keirsey and Marilyn Bates (Prometheus Nemesis, 1984).

This is one of the most popular and accessible books for understanding various personality types. You begin by completing a questionnaire (which is adapted from the Myers-Briggs Type Indicator) to determine which of the sixteen types fits your personality. The book provides a useful vocabulary and phraseology for having a meaningful and productive discussion of how your differences in personality complement one another.

The Intimacy Factor by David and Jan Stoop (Thomas Nelson, 1993).

Do you really know what type of personality you have? Or what type your spouse has? Does your personality really affect the intimacy you achieve in a relationship? These are the questions this book answers. Based primarily on the popular Myers-Briggs Type Indicator, it explores the differences between extroverts and introverts, thinking and feeling, judging and perceiving, and so on. All the while, the Stoops are showing how our personalities affect our ability to love and be loved.

Chapter Eleven:
Questions About Sex

I enjoy making love with my husband, but he believes sex is much more important to our marriage than I do. He views it as a sign of how well we are doing as a couple. Is there any truth to this idea?

Sex is critically important for a quality marriage. We'll say it again. Sex makes a significant impact on whether you will rate your marriage as satisfying or not.

Several studies confirm that sexual satisfaction and marital satisfaction go together. In one survey on the importance of sex for marriage, the results were compelling: Couples who rated their sex lives positively also rated their marriages positively, and those who rated their sex lives negatively rated their marriages negatively as well.[1] In other words, if couples report that sex is unimportant to them, it is very likely that they view their entire marriage as unhappy. Both the quantity and quality of sex in marriage are central to a good overall relationship.

In a landmark study of American couples, it was found that the frequency of marital sexual interactions was strongly associated with how the over seven thousand married respondents rated their sexual satisfaction.[2] Nine out of ten of the couples who were having sex three or more times a week reported satisfaction with the quality of their sex lives. In contrast, only half of those individuals who were having sex one to four times a month were satisfied. Furthermore, only a third of those with frequency rates of once a month or less reported satisfaction.

You might be relieved to know that a number of factors other than frequency of sexual interaction have also been linked to satisfaction with marital sex. Mutuality in initiating sex can be an important contributor to sexual satisfaction of both wives and husbands. It also appears that women who take an active role during sexual sharing are more likely to be pleased with their sex lives than those who assume a more passive role.[3]

No study states that a high quality sex life is an absolute requirement for a high quality marriage, nor that a good sex life guarantees a good marriage. Nonetheless, studies consistently suggest that quality of sex and quality of marriage do go together in most cases.

When we first got married we had sex much more frequently. Through the years, we have kind of settled into a pattern of making love only two or three times a month, and we wonder if that's normal. How many times in a month does the average couple have sex?

For most couples, achieving a satisfying marriage depends a great deal on the development of a pattern of mutually satisfying, frequent sex. Despite the general knowledge that "sex is important to marriage," recently married couples have few guidelines about "how often is often enough." As a result each couple negotiates its own guidelines as part of building their family culture during the first years of marriage.

A study of couples in the early years of marriage found that different couples came to widely varying conclusions about the frequency of sex in marriage.[4] While some couples had intercourse an average of once a week, others reportedly did so an average of more than once a day. Clearly, four times a month to forty-five times a month is a very broad range. But a number of studies confirm that newly married couples have widely divergent frequency rates.

What about the "average" newly married couple? Couples married one year or less average fifteen times a month. And a study of couples married two years or less found that about half had sex three or more times a week while the other half had sex less than three times a week.[5] Based on these results, the average couple has sexual intercourse about fifteen times a month during the early years of marriage.

After the first year or so, most married couples have sexual intercourse less often. In one study, for example, thirty percent of the couples maintained or increased their first year's sexual intercourse rate into the second year, but fully seventy percent experienced declines, ranging from small to drastic, in frequency of intercourse.[6]

Why the decline? Increasing age, with an accompanying decline in sexual interest, is, of course, one possible explanation. However, the decline cannot be attributed solely to the aging process since it occurs regardless of how young or how old the partners are when they marry. When married couples are asked to explain the decline of sexual frequency in their own marriages, they typically point to four types of factors: pregnancy and fear of becoming pregnant, work, children, and availability.[7]

Regardless of how frequently you have sex with your spouse, the goal is not to reach a "magic" number. What matters most is that the two of you are working at a mutually satisfying pattern that does not become taken for granted.

After a couple of years of marriage, it has become obvious to us that we not only have different ideas about how frequently we should make love, but we also have different sexual needs. How do we each get our sexual needs met?

Great sex is not built on instincts. Just as couples need to acquire skills for relating and communicating, so too do they need to learn skills for sex.

Men and women have different sexual needs, and one of the best ways of discovering these with your partner is through open and honest communication during sexual play. For a variety of reasons, however, many couples never get around to talking about their differences. Some couples go years without ever understanding some of the most fundamental and unique sexual needs between the genders. What follows are some basic principles that can help you and your spouse enjoy more satisfaction in the bedroom. You will do your sex life a great favor to not only read through them but discuss them with your partner as well.

WHAT MEN NEED TO KNOW ABOUT WOMEN

Women, unlike men, do not separate sex from the relational and emotional aspects of the relationship. They want a sense of connection that is experienced for more than an hour before sex is initiated. They want an overarching atmosphere of intimacy and affection built on daily choices. As one author put it, "Sex begins in the kitchen." For this reason, it is critically important to communicate in loving ways throughout the day and give your wife special attention. For women, sex has much more to it than physical arousal.

Your wife is also more vulnerable to distraction when it comes to sex. If she is fatigued, feeling hurt, or struggling with her body image, she may have difficulty focusing on her sexual drive. So do your best to minimize distractions by paying attention to what dampens her sexual desires.

After a man has had an orgasm, he requires some recuperative time. Women, on the other hand, can have a series of orgasms, one right after the other (as many as five or more separate orgasms in a couple of minutes). Some men, wanting to be "the world's greatest lover," get hung up on keeping track of their wives' orgasms. That's the wrong approach. Focus on helping your wife enjoy the sexual experience, and let go of keeping score.

WHAT WOMEN NEED TO KNOW ABOUT MEN

Men, unlike women, often view making love as a primary way of connecting with their mates. In other words, their sexual activity can stem from an inability to connect in other ways, like conversations and nonsexual touching. For this reason your husband's sex drive may be more apparent than yours. If so, enjoy it as you allow yourselves to tap into your sexual desire.

Men are geared more than women for immediate gratification. If he sees you getting ready for a party and it turns him on, he probably won't be satisfied with a long kiss and a few caresses. You may be thinking about being late to the party or messing up your lipstick, but he loves the excitement of the moment, even if brief. This may not be your idea of an ideal sexual encounter with your mate, but sometimes accommodating his quickness is a loving gift that he will appreciate as much as you enjoy the more leisurely approach.

You have undoubtedly noticed that your husband is prone to visual stimulation. It serves as a sexual cue to him. For example, you may seldom notice your husband getting out of the shower, but he notices you. He can become aroused by catching a quick glimpse of you on an exercise machine or even doing something as mundane as a simple chore. It often takes very little for your husband to become aroused because he is more visually oriented than you. So be ready for the unexpected and relish his attraction toward you.

The bottom line in getting your sexual needs met is to assume that your partner doesn't know how to satisfy you. Beginning with this premise may help you ask for what you would like. That's the key, and research bears it out. In one survey, eighty-eight percent of the women who reported always discussing their sexual feelings with their spouses described their sex lives as good or very good. In contrast, only thirty percent of the women who reported never discussing sex with their partners described their sex lives as good or very good.[8]

Remember, what makes each of you happy is not necessarily the same thing. Your needs, in fact, may be dramatically different. So do not make the mistake of assuming your partner knows how to meet your sexual needs if you do not talk to each other about them.

My sex drive is definitely stronger than my wife's, and that sometimes causes conflict in our relationship. It's not like I can change my urges. What can we do when our sex drives differ?

It is not uncommon for couples to feel out of sync when it comes to the desire and frequency of lovemaking. Differing desires seem to be part of many marriages. Here are some strategies for both of you.

For the partner with a lesser desire for sex:

1. *Keep your life in balance.* Sometimes a low sexual desire can be a reflection of feeling stressed out and unusually busy, flustered, and harried. So take a good look at your daily activities to be sure you are maintaining balance. Take care to create a life that is full and interesting but not overly hectic and stressful.

2. *Pay attention to subtle sexual cues.* Unlike your partner, you may never experience a strong burst of sexual desire, so you may need to amplify the sexy feeling you do have. When you feel even the slightest twinge of desire, follow through on it. If

certain conditions make you a bit more receptive to lovemaking, take advantage of them.

3. *When you need to say no, don't feel guilty.* If you make an effort to meet your partner's needs much of the time, don't blame yourself for those times when you choose not to. You can help ease the "rejection" by simply postponing your lovemaking to a later time when you are more in the mood.

4. *Accept more responsibility for your own arousal.* Don't expect your partner to read your mind. If you want more hugging and kissing, then ask for it. Because you have less spontaneous desire, you must learn how to create it. Initiate those activities you find arousing.

For the partner with a greater desire for sex:

1. *Learn what makes your partner excited.* The more adept you are at arousing your spouse, the more often you'll both be excited. Be patient and take time to listen and learn what your partner enjoys most about sex. Ask gentle questions to help you truly discover your partner's pleasures.

2. *Respect your partner's preconditions for lovemaking.* Maybe your spouse only likes to have sex at night with the lights off. If that's what he or she enjoys, honor that. The time of day may not make much difference to you, but your partner will be more responsive if you pay attention to it.

3. *Don't take rejection personally.* Sometimes the spouse who gets turned down for lovemaking suffers tremendous feelings of rejection. Don't allow your ego to get bruised when this happens to you. It's likely to be the result of a number of factors that have nothing to do with you.

If these suggestions do not help the two of you work out a mutually satisfying sexual relationship, don't give up. This part of your marriage is too important to neglect. Consider seeing an objective professional counselor or sex therapist who can advise you on your specific circumstances.

We have tried a couple of different methods of birth control and still haven't found a method we really like. In fact, we are not even sure of all our options. What can you tell us about the different kinds of contraceptives?

In certain periods of American history, only sexual activities that could result in reproduction were encouraged; sexual behavior intended solely for pleasure was prohibited or discouraged. This is no longer the case. In fact, the major impetus behind most sexual activity today is pleasure. This, of course, means that there is a very high probability that a couple's actions will result in pregnancy unless they take special measures. Without these special measures, nine out of ten sexually active, fertile women can expect to become pregnant within one year.

The "special measures" sexually active couples take to prevent or lessen the probability of pregnancy are known collectively as contraception (literally, "against conception"). What contraceptive methods do modern couples use? How effective are these methods? The following chart will answer these questions and many more.[9] It lists the particular contraceptive method and gives a brief description of how it prevents conception. In addition, the chart provides estimates of costs, advantages and disadvantages, and the method's effectiveness.

Decisions about contraception are not easy, and fear of an unwanted pregnancy can negatively affect both partners' sexual experience. By the way, a husband should take an active interest in the contraception used, otherwise his wife may resent the fact that she is carrying the entire responsibility for the decision. If you talk openly about sharing the responsibility of birth control, it will enhance your relationship.

Method	How It Works	Effectiveness	Yearly Cost	Advantages	Disadvantages
Withdrawal	Male withdraws penis from female's vagina prior to ejaculation	Poor to fair	None	No cost	Requires high motivation
Rhythm	Couple avoids penis-vagina contact during female's fertile period after careful observations of her cycle	Poor to fair	None	No cost	Requires high motivation, prolonged abstinence
Condom	Rubber sheath placed over penis so that semen cannot enter vagina	Good	$75	Easy to use	Interference with coitus
Diaphragm with spermicide	Rubber cup, fitted over cervix, holds spermidical cream or jelly which kills sperm trying to enter	Poor to fair	$175	No side effects	Remains in place up to 12 hours; must be fitted by physician; aesthetic objections
Cervical cap with spermicide	Miniature diaphragm with a tall dome; creates airtight seal around cervical opening, preventing sperm passage	Poor to fair	$175	Can remain in place up to 48 hours; no side effects	Must be fitted by physician
Vaginal foam and suppositories	Spermicidal foam inserted into vagina keeps sperm from entering cervix and kills them	Poor to fair	$75	Easy to use	Messy
Sponge	Doughnut-shaped, polyurethane sponge, presaturated with spermicide, placed at cervical entrance, forms barrier over cervix and continually releases spermicide	Very poor to fair	$250	Easy to use	Continual expense
Female condom	Seven-inch-long transparent plastic bag with flexible ring inside closed upper end, and another flexible ring at open bottom and end	Poor to fair	$350	Easy to use; no side effects	Interferes with coitus; continual expense
Hormone birth control pills	Female body is hormonally "tricked" so that ovary is prevented from releasing monthly egg	Excellent	$300	Highly effective; not used at time of coitus	Cost; possible side effects; must be taken daily
Progestin-only birth control pills	Same	Excellent	$300	Highly effective	Same
Norplant	Tiny rods of hormones implanted under female's skin which prevent ovulation; works for five-year period	Excellent	$500	Highly effective; automatic; semipermanent; reversible	Some side effects

Early in our marriage, I had pain in my vagina while we were having intercourse. And occasionally my husband cannot maintain an erection while we are making love. We understand that these are fairly common problems, but we are wondering what other sexual struggles couples cope with. What are the most common sexual problems?

Human sexuality is complex, incorporating both physical and psychological components. If sexual organs are not in working order or if psychological factors make it difficult to become sexually aroused, individuals may be unable to achieve sexual pleasure. Many people, even those deeply in love with their spouse, are troubled by sexual problems at some time during their lives.

The most common sexual problems for females are inhibited sexual desire, dyspareunia, and anorgasmia. Males with sexual problems are most often troubled by inhibited sexual desire, impotence, and premature ejaculation.

Inhibited sexual desire (ISD) refers to a lack of sexual interest or desire. Surveys have found that as many as one in three women and one in six men complain of lack of sexual desire.[10] In some cases, physical factors such as hormonal imbalances, health problems, and the use of birth control pills contribute to ISD. In other cases, social or psychological circumstances such as being tired, overworked, depressed, or under stress result in sexual disinterest.

Dyspareunia is the condition of feeling pain during intercourse. For women, the pain is felt in the vagina. Men with prostate problems, infections, or allergic reactions to certain contraceptives may also experience painful intercourse. Sometimes painful intercourse for women is the result of a painful spasm of the outer third of the vagina and an involuntary tightening of vaginal muscles that make penetration by the penis extremely painful (this is knows as vaginismus).

Anorgasmia is the inability to have an orgasm. The problem is fairly common among women but rare among men. Sex experts estimate that five to ten percent of all women over twenty-five have not yet learned how to have an orgasm and that another twenty percent have orgasms only sporadically.[11] The ability to reach orgasm is often a matter of learning and practice. Lack of factual knowledge about sexuality, the absence of a warm, supportive spouse, or a partner who ejaculates prematurely can prevent a woman from learning to have an orgasm.

Impotence is the inability to have an erection or to maintain one long enough to have intercourse. There are no accurate statistics of the prevalence of impotence, but experts estimate that as many as one out of every ten men has some type of impotence problem.[12] Impotence can be either temporary or permanent. Certain prescription medications (antidepressants, antihypertensives, and so forth) are associated with impotence in men. Permanent impotence is considered infrequent, especially among young males.

Premature ejaculation is the inability of a male to control the ejaculatory reflex. Premature ejaculation is considered a sexual dysfunction if the male has an orgasm without any sense of control "too quickly" after initiating intercourse. It is almost always psychologically based, especially for males who have never learned to control the timing of their orgasm. For those males who at one time could control the timing of their orgasm and who have lost that control, physical factors (disease or neurological damage) may be involved. An estimated thirty-six to thirty-eight percent of males experience premature ejaculation, with those under twenty-five most often affected.

The treatment of sexual problems varies with the particular problem and the person. Medical doctors, particularly those with some training in treating sexual disorders, should be consulted first to determine if the sexual problem is physical in nature. Some sexual problems can be treated with medication. Sex therapists and other counselors can also be of help with a variety of sexual problems (see "Questions About Getting Help" in this book for more information on this).

One of my biggest fears is that my husband will have an affair. I have no objective grounds to suspect this, and I don't think I'm paranoid, but it's just that there are so many stories of this happening to couples. What can we do to protect our marriage against extramarital affairs?

People enter into extramarital relationships for a variety of reasons. Sometimes they are motivated by excitement or variety. Some are motivated by a desire to "prove" to themselves that they are desirable to the opposite sex. In other cases, people may be dissatisfied with their marriage and use an affair to hurt their spouse. In such instances the offending party may be quite indiscreet to ensure that the "wronged" spouse will discover the infidelity. Whatever the reasons for affairs, every couple must consider themselves at risk to some degree or another.

It is difficult to estimate the prevalence of extramarital affairs, but some surveys have reported that about half of all married men and a quarter of married women admitted to extramarital sexual intercourse at least once by age forty.[13] Experts see few signs that this disturbing trend will diminish.

What can couples do to protect their marriage against the irreversible damage of infidelity? Christian counselor and author of *Broken Promises* Henry Virkler believes that a first step is becoming aware of several common myths couples carry about affairs.[14] Such beliefs, often held by Christians, are:

1. *The majority of affairs start because of lust.* The truth is that most affairs, especially for women, occur because of unmet emotional needs for friendship and security.

2. *A strong personal faith in Christ inoculates a person against an affair.* A personal faith may reduce to some degree the likelihood of an affair, but the inoculation is far from one hundred percent effective.

3. *We don't really need to worry about an affair in our marriage because they rarely happen in good marriages.* Again, a good

marriage may reduce the chances of an affair, but it cannot be taken for granted.

4. *A man having an affair will almost always choose a lover who is physically more attractive than his wife.* This false belief is connected to the idea that sex is the most important ingredient in an affair.

5. *When a spouse's affair is discovered, it is best for the offended party to pretend not to know, and thereby avoid a crisis.* This approach is often taken out of fear of the consequences, but if the behavior is not confronted, it very likely will be repeated again and again.

After facing up to these common misbeliefs, a couple can further protect their marriage against an affair by identifying the kinds of situations in which each is the most vulnerable and come up with a plan to avoid such circumstances. For example, maybe going to a business lunch with a person of the opposite sex is not a good idea. In such cases, you could always be sure to include another associate, bring up your affection for your spouse in the conversation, and so on. The idea is to plan beforehand ways of avoiding circumstances that hold the slightest possibility for infidelity. You might consider making a pact with each other to draw a line for physical contact with others or to never share love language with someone other than your mate (including a note or card or even a phone call just to talk).[15] Without a conscious intention, some behavior can unintentionally draw two people into an affair.

One more thought. Whenever a couple is experiencing a developmental transition (such as moving to a new location, starting a new job, the birth of a child) and their lives are more unstable and unpredictable than usual, it is important to work at staying connected at an emotional and physical level. These difficult times are often when couples let their guard down and open themselves up to temptation.

My wife was sexually abused as a child, and it seems to affect our marriage in a number of ways, not least of which is our sex life. What can we expect from this situation, and what can we do to help it?

We recently counseled a couple in your same shoes. She was the victim of repeated sexual abuse by a teenage boy who babysat her off and on for a couple of years. The memories of these terrible incidents are seared into her mind, and it often takes very little for them to come flooding over her present-day experiences. As you know, this can be heart-wrenching to observe and, in the case of this couple at least, extremely frustrating.

Recent surveys estimate that one out of three girls experiences a sexually traumatizing incident by the time she is seventeen.[16] These tragic wounds, of course, interfere tremendously with the ability to relate intimately during lovemaking with a spouse. Both childhood sexual abuse and adult sexual assault greatly interfere with married sex.

Female as well as male sexual abuse survivors often suffer from problems with trust, safety, and shame. Incest experiences of more than thirty years ago, for example, can govern current patterns of their sexuality. Because of sexual abuse, sexual activity in marriage can become associated with emotional and often physical pain.

Research has shown that women with a history of childhood sexual abuse are more likely than other women to have chronic pelvic pain and to experience depression, anxiety, and low self-esteem.[17] In addition, sexual abuse survivors often experience specific aversion reactions to exactly what was done to them during the sexual assault. They will have "flashbacks," sudden images of the smells, sounds, sights, feelings, or other reminders of the sexual abuse. These reminders may dramatically interrupt any positive feelings and pleasure the sexual abuse survivor is experiencing at the time. In some cases, a sexual abuse survivor may have symptoms of fear or aversion to sexual contact yet have little memory of sexual abuse. As an unconscious self-protective mechanism, victims may even repress memories of the trauma; they simply have symptoms when they are with their spouse that they cannot explain or understand.[18]

If your partner or you have suffered sexual abuse, you have undoubtedly experienced confusion, feelings of rejection, and plenty of anger. Perhaps your sex life has been dampened to near nonexistence. Whatever your current situation, here are a few pointers that may be of some help.

FOR THE VICTIMIZED SURVIVOR

While you may be viewed as the person with the "problem," and while you may feel like a patient who needs to be treated and healed, you are not helpless. There are several things you can do to help your spouse. For starters, you can affirm the commitment you have toward your partner and your marriage. Even though sex may be difficult, you can offer whatever other kinds of physical affection you can. You can also remind your partner that your difficulty with sex stems from the abuse, not from his or her attractiveness or ability as a lover. In addition, you can recognize and appreciate all that your partner is doing to help bring about healing for you. Express appreciation as often as you can. He or she may have moments of impatience or exasperation, but focus on positive efforts when they occur. Finally, be as open as possible with your partner on what is going on inside of you.

FOR THE SPOUSE OF THE SURVIVOR

Above all, be patient. We have seen too many couples in this situation self-destruct because the spouse of the survivor does not take the time to understand and truly comprehend the ramifications of a partner's abuse. Empathize with your spouse. Ask questions. And reassure your partner that abuse will never have to be endured again. Also, respect your partner's right to say no and set sexual limits (something they didn't have in the abusive situation). Another powerful way you can help your partner grow beyond disabling shame and guilt is to place the blame and responsibility for the abuse on the perpetrator. Your mate was a victim who did not choose to be victimized even though he or she will be tempted to feel guilty for it. You play a very special role in helping your partner find healing. Take your role seriously and do all you can to walk the healing journey together.

While you and your partner can do a great deal together in coping with the fallout of sexual abuse, there may come a time when you need more objective intervention. A competent professional counselor can do a great deal to help you speed up the healing process, so investigate this possibility to see how it might help you and your marriage.

What are some of the most helpful resources on sexuality and marriage?

Getting Your Sex Life Off to a Great Start: A Guide for Engaged and Newlywed Couples by Clifford and Joyce Penner (Word, 1994).

Intelligent, deliberate preparation for a lifetime of sexual pleasure is a worthy investment, and this book is an excellent guide to doing just that. Renowned sexual counselors and best-selling authors Cliff and Joyce Penner take you through an encouraging process that begins by dispelling sexual myths and then guides you in getting to know yourself and each other emotionally and physically. With reassuring enthusiasm and straightforward advice, the Penners show you how to clarify your expectations and pursue true marital passion through creative, step-by-step exercises and easy-to-understand examples.

The Gift of Sex: A Guide to Sexual Fulfillment by Clifford and Joyce Penner (Word, 1981).

This is an ideal guide for understanding your own sexuality and the sexual relationship in marriage with all its pleasure, drive, frustration, and fulfillment. The book focuses on the physical dimension (how our bodies work), the total experience (having fun, pleasuring, stimulating, etc.), moving past sexual barriers (differing sexual needs), resolving technical difficulties (no arousal, pain, etc.), and finding help, all from a thoroughly Christian perspective built on the premise that sexuality is a gift from God. The Penners have included well over a dozen sexual enhancement exercises that have proven helpful to thousands of married couples. The book is readable, practical, frank, and intimate.

A Celebration of Sex: A Christian Couple's Manual by Douglas E. Rosenau (Thomas Nelson, 1994).

This thorough book provides assistance on dozens of sexual issues and answers specific, often unasked questions about sexual topics. It presents all married couples with detailed techniques and behavioral skills for a full awareness and understanding of sexual pleasure. One of the strengths of this volume is the inclusion of several detailed diagrams and illustrations. The goal of *A Celebration of Sex* is to help you create the one-flesh union that God has ordained, the spiritual merger of wife and husband.

The Sexual Man by Archibald D. Hart (Word, 1994).

This is an honest, carefully documented book that answers dozens of questions about today's men and their sexuality. Dr. Hart has surveyed more than six hundred men to discover what satisfies men sexually, what sexual fears and failures haunt them, and the keys to a fulfilled and guilt-free sex life. This book, however, is not for men only. Every wife can learn more about her partner by reading these pages that are packed with helpful charts depicting male sexuality.

Your Wife Was Sexually Abused by John Courtright and Sid Rogers (Zondervan, 1994).

If your wife has been sexually abused, this little book is a must. Written by two men who have had to deal with their own wives' past sexual abuse, this book will help you find healing amidst the pain and confusion. Each heart-moving chapter includes questions for thought and discussion that will help you work through your own personal situation to a healthy and stable marriage.

Chapter Twelve:
Questions About Spiritual Matters

Both my husband and I were raised in Christian homes and are committed believers. We go to church almost every week and have plenty of couple friends who do the same. Is there anything more to being spiritually intimate as a married couple?

Happily married couples eventually discover an innate longing to bond with their lover, not just for comfort, not just for passion, but also for meaning. Of course, in our busy culture, couples can avoid the pursuit of spiritual meaning by remaining on the surface—staying too busy for soul-searching—but for couples who are willing to venture into the deep, a rich reward is waiting.

The spiritual dimension is the most important and least talked about aspect of a healthy marriage. While every individual must come to an understanding of life's meaning alone, couples must also discover the meaning of their marriage together. In a very real sense, the soul of your marriage needs to be nourished, for whether you cultivate spiritual intimacy in your marriage or not could be the most significant determiner of the success and quality of your relationship.

Researchers have studied the effect of spirituality on marriage, and they consistently find a strong and positive connection between religion and marital harmony, but only if the couple's religion is built on spiritual well-being. What is meant by spiritual well-being? It comes down to whether the couple bases their religion on what is called an "internal orientation" or an "external orientation." A person with an internal orientation to religion views religion as a goal in itself, while someone with an external orientation views religion as a tool to be used as a means to another end, such as increasing participation in social events.[1] Healthy spirituality is not incorporated into a marriage because it brings a social support system or something to do on Sunday morning. Healthy spirituality is built on a conviction of the heart and a personal relationship with God. It transcends treating church as a country club for activity and social gathering and views it as a means to worshiping the Creator. Allow us to say it in plain language: A couple with an external orientation to religion will seldom enjoy the real blessings of healthy spiritual well-being.

So don't take your religious activity for granted. Don't think that just because you attend church together as a couple you can check "spiritual well-being" off your marital to-do list. True spirituality goes much deeper. It involves seeking to walk as Jesus walked, and a desire to know and love God—not just as individuals, but as a couple. Spiritual intimacy is like yeast in a loaf of bread. It will ultimately determine whether your marriage rises successfully or falls disappointingly flat.

Before we got married, we would often read the Bible and pray together. We've tried to keep that up in the last two years of our marriage, but it's not working. How can we have a consistent and meaningful devotional time together?

Ask most long-standing Christian couples you know and respect how you build a satisfactory devotional life and they will probably tell you "over time." In fact, we have asked dozens of Christian leaders how they cultivate spiritual intimacy in their marriage, and nearly every one of them has carved out a unique path that fits their particular style.

What we are saying is that there is no one single right way for building a consistent and meaningful quiet time. There are no "three easy steps" to follow that work for everyone.

For several years early in our marriage we worked at reading the Bible together each day. We failed miserably and often felt guilty because of it. Today we have a pattern that works for now, but it will change. All of the couples we surveyed said their devotional life together is evolving. What matters to us, and the couples we have talked to, is that deliberate energy is being spent on nurturing the marital soul. For us, that generally means that we are working primarily on three classic spiritual disciplines.

First, we focus on worship together. Both of us have gone to church since we were children, and we can often take worship at church for granted. It is easy to just attend church week after week without making a conscious effort to see that we are doing this as a married couple, that worshiping together is a vital part of nourishing our married soul. Worship has a way of transforming relationships. To stand before the Holy One of eternity is to grow and change—together. In worship, God's transforming power makes its way into our hearts and gives us a renewed capacity to love one another.

Second, we focus on shared service. Something wonderful happens when a couple reaches out to others as a team. Almost mystically the act of service bonds them together. Reaching out promotes sharing and compassion that is reflected back into one's marriage. There are hundreds of ways to incorporate shared service into your marriage: volunteering at a retirement center, teaching a Sunday school class, supporting a Third World child, being generous with needy people in your church, opening your home for hospitality to others, and so on. The key is finding something that fits your personal style as a couple. You might try reaching out to someone as a team and then keep it your secret.

Third, we focus on prayer. Couples who frequently pray together are twice as likely as those who pray less often to describe their marriages as being highly romantic. Maybe you are thinking, *Of course prayer is important, why even mention it?* We mention it because we have seen dozens of spiritually devout couples who are active in their church and committed to their faith who never seem to get around to praying together as a couple. And no amount of being "religious" can make up for the time couples spend in shared prayer. So we urge you to pray in a way that is meaningful to both of you. Maybe that means saying the Lord's Prayer together, or simple sentence prayers, or even silent prayers together. The form of your prayers is not nearly as important as the act of having a prayer time together.

Of course there are plenty of other helpful things couples might do to cultivate spiritual intimacy, but we have found that focusing primarily on worship, shared service, and prayer are critical. We have also learned that for us it is best to think in terms of having a quiet time on a weekly rather than a daily schedule. Of course, we maintain our individual walks with the Lord on a daily basis and we each pray for one another daily, but our soul-to-soul time comes weekly. That's not for everyone, but it works for us. In fact, our devotional book, *Becoming Soul Mates*, is structured this way. Couples who use it say the weekly schedule is less guilt-inducing and more meaningful for them than a daily schedule.

Still, it all comes back to finding a pattern that works for both of you. You will probably try a variety of strategies before you lock onto one that works best. That's all part of the journey of becoming soul mates.

We moved to a new city recently and want to find a church home that we both appreciate. We've shopped around a little bit, but so far we haven't found a church where we both want to get involved. What suggestions do you have on choosing a church together?

Finding a church you both feel good about and giving your time and resources to make it work is vital to the spiritual health of your marriage. The following guidelines may help you in that process.

1. *Be a good "consumer" when you're church shopping.* Many couples choose a church because of its location or its architecture or any number of superficial reasons. Don't make the mistake of not looking for a church that shows real signs of health. In *A Faith That Hurts, a Faith That Heals*, Stephen Arterburn and Jack Felton describe a healthy church as one which is not controlling, blaming, delusional, distrustful, and so on. Make your own list of what you want in a church and shop around.

2. *Remember that there is no perfect church.* Once you have made a list of what you are looking for in a church, you may end up hunting long and hard and still come up empty if you do not remind yourself that no church is perfect. Every church is going to have deficits. Even the spectacularly successful Jerusalem church in the book of Acts had occasional problems, and yours won't do better than that. So don't waste your time looking for perfection.

3. *Establish a natural pattern of attendance.* Once you have settled into a church home, make it a consistent part of your life together. Don't fall into the weekly debate of "Shall we go or not?" Instead, think of church attendance as a necessary fueling station for your soul. Just as your automobile needs to be refilled with gasoline, so does your relationship with God need to be tuned up at church.

4. *Support your church financially.* If you are attending a church regularly, you need to contribute to its ongoing ministry in your life and marriage. That means tithing your income. You can make this a regular part of your budget and pay it just as you would any other expense. Supporting the work of the church not only helps the church, it helps you and your marriage to invest in something important too.

5. *Try to find one area where you can serve together.* Many Christian couples arrive at church and head in separate directions, each to their own areas of involvement. While you may certainly have some independent realms of service, try to get involved in some team ministry. Whether teaching a class, singing together in the choir, or codirecting an outreach ministry, look for something that brings you together in the house of God.

6. *Maintain a healthy balance.* While it is critically valuable to find a place of service together, it is equally important not to overdo it. We have seen plenty of couples who get so involved in their church that they lose touch with each other. You need to have time in your week that is just for you, time that is not spent giving, but receiving from one another. If you find that your church activities keep you from having family time together, you know you have crossed the line and it is time to realign your priorities.

7. *Don't bad-mouth the church.* Since no church, no matter how great, is perfect, you don't need to spend time griping about this and that. You don't even need to point out the flaws together. Not that you shouldn't think critically about your church and its actions, but you don't need to nitpick. Make it a standard practice to discuss problems you see only with those in the church who can make a difference, and work from the assumption that your fellow members and leaders are well-meaning. Of course, if you are going to gripe about a problem, you should be the first one volunteering to make an improvement.

I am a committed Christian and my husband isn't. Shortly after we got married, I gave my life to Christ when a friend invited me to her church. Since then I have been involved in a weekly Bible study for women and long to go to church with my husband. Needless to say, he is very skeptical and refuses to go. What can I do?

One of the most difficult situations a Christian ever faces is being married to a person who is not a believer. If this is your predicament, you have undoubtedly experienced tension and anguish on many levels. However, there are some principles an "unequally yoked" spouse can learn and apply that will make life easier.

The first principle is to respect your spouse. "Mutual respect" is essential to the health of your marriage. While disagreeing with and debating a spouse's worldview might be tempting, punching holes in a partner's belief system is seldom productive. "It is critically important to show my husband respect," one woman told us. "If I don't respect him as a person, how can I expect my children to respect their father?" Sure, you might want to point out what your spouse is missing by not accepting Christ, but these kinds of messages are better heard when they come from a foundation of respect. The main point, however, is that if you show respect to your partner, you are much more likely to get respect back in return. As Henry Ward Beecher once said, "If you want someone to see what Christ will do for him, let him see what Christ has done for you."

Your partner is far more likely to be open about faith issues if he knows you are not setting him up to look or feel foolish. To build this kind of foundation, you may want to take a moment to make a list of qualities you respect about your spouse. What characteristics in him or her do you admire? You may also want to think about how you show your partner respect. To take this exercise a step further, ask yourself how your partner would answer this same question. Jo Berry, author of the helpful book *Beloved Unbeliever: Loving Your Husband into the Faith*, reminds her readers again and again not to get lost in the negatives.[2]

While your partner's lack of personal faith creates a spiritual gap in your relationship, you still have much in common. That is the focus of the second principle: to keep in mind your common ground. If you have lost sight of this shared vision, take time to rediscover it. Talk about what values you both hold. What principles do you both want to live by? If you are like most couples, you agree on many of the basics even if your spouse doesn't put the principles in a Christian context.

We would be remiss if I did not mention a principle that every wise person understands—prayer. You can pray that your spouse will be filled with questions for which only God has answers: that he or she will be drawn to the Lord and that you will be strengthened and guided to be a good Christian role model for your spouse. Prayer in its simplest definition is merely a wish turned Godward. And according to George MacDonald, "Anything large enough for a wish to light upon is large enough to hang a prayer on." So turn your wishes toward God. Raise your thoughts to heaven.

Above all, remember that God has placed you in a unique position of being his representative to the person you love. Don't take this position lightly. And don't give up hope.

I'm in a men's accountability group at my church, and someone in that group said the Bible has very little to say about marriage. I disagreed with him, but lately began thinking that maybe he was right. Can you help me solve this question? Does the Bible have anything practical to say about marriage?

We often hear this question from couples when we start talking about spirituality and marriage. And we are glad for it because the Bible is filled with pearls of wisdom and knowledge on marriage. It provides a great deal of valuable guidance and instruction in very practical terms. A small sampling of the verses that address marriage begins on the next page. We pray that these verses will serve as a springboard to motivate you in searching the inspired writings of Scripture to uncover many more of its practical offerings on marriage.

So they are no longer two, but one. Therefore what God has joined together, let man not separate.

MARK 10:8–9

A gentle answer turns away wrath, but a harsh word stirs up anger.

PROVERBS 15:1

Husbands, love your wives and do not be harsh with them.

COLOSSIANS 3:19

A wife of noble character is her husband's crown, but a disgraceful wife is like decay in his bones.

PROVERBS 12:4

Pleasant words are a honeycomb, sweet to the soul and healing to the bones.

PROVERBS 16:24

But at the beginning of creation God "made them male and female."

MARK 10:6

A word aptly spoken is like apples of gold in settings of silver.

PROVERBS 25:11

Husbands, love your wives, just as Christ loved the church and gave himself up for her to make her holy.

EPHESIANS 5:25–26

He who answers before listening—that is his folly and shame.

PROVERBS 18:13

Do not be yoked together with unbelievers. For what do righteousness and wickedness have in common? Or what fellowship can light have with darkness?

2 CORINTHIANS 6:14

Starting a quarrel is like breaching a dam; so drop the matter before a dispute breaks out.

PROVERBS 17:14

The wife's body does not belong to her alone but also to her husband. In the same way, the husband's body does not belong to him alone but also to his wife.

1 CORINTHIANS 7:4

As charcoal to embers and as wood to fire, so is a quarrelsome man for kindling strife.

PROVERBS 26:21

Love does not delight in evil but rejoices with the truth. It always protects, always trusts, always hopes, always perseveres.

1 CORINTHIANS 13:6–7

Marriage should be honored by all, and the marriage bed kept pure, for God will judge the adulterer and all the sexually immoral.

HEBREWS 13:4

Husbands ought to love their wives as their own bodies. He who loves his wife loves himself.

EPHESIANS 5:28

A quarrelsome wife is like a constant dripping.

PROVERBS 19:13

In the same way, their wives are to be women worthy of respect, not malicious talkers but temperate and trustworthy in everything.

1 TIMOTHY 3:11

So in everything, do to others what you would have them do to you.

MATTHEW 7:12

Better a dry crust with peace and quiet than a house full of feasting, with strife.

PROVERBS 17:1

Husbands, in the same way be considerate as you live with your wives, and treat them with respect as the weaker partner and as heirs with you of the gracious gift of life, so that nothing will hinder your prayers.

1 PETER 3:7

Charm is deceptive, and beauty is fleeting; but a woman who fears the LORD is to be praised.

PROVERBS 31:30

For this reason a man will leave his father and mother and be united to his wife, and the two will become one flesh.

MARK 10:7–8

A cheerful look brings joy to the heart, and good news gives health to the bones.

PROVERBS 15:30

A gift given in secret soothes anger.

PROVERBS 21:14

What are some of the most helpful resources on spiritual matters in marriage?

Marriage Spirituality: Ten Disciplines for Couples Who Love God by Paul Stevens (InterVarsity Press, 1989).

Paul Stevens begins with the premise that we do not have to develop our spirituality alone, as if we were all monks. He presents ten spiritual disciplines in this book that every couple can practice together. From prayer to service, conversation to confession, each of these disciplines strengthens both faith and marriage. In the context of each chapter you will discover not only solid biblical principles but many practical suggestions as well.

The Spiritually Intimate Marriage: Discover the Close Relationship God Has Designed for Every Couple by Donald Harvey (Revell, 1991).

Drawing from case studies and his own personal experience to define spiritual intimacy, Donald Harvey identifies problems that inhibit closeness and offers counsel for working with a mate who isn't ready for a deeper level of intimacy. This book will show you how to take the steps necessary to develop a spiritual growth plan uniquely your own.

Experiencing God Together by David Stoop (Tyndale, 1996).

This book begins with a "Spiritual Inventory" for couples to assess their spiritual life. Next, it covers topics such as prayer, submission, worship, service, confession, forgiveness, and the need for long-term spiritual exercise. This book will strengthen your marriage by helping you develop spiritual intimacy.

Becoming Soul Mates: Cultivating Spiritual Intimacy in the Early Years of Marriage by Les and Leslie Parrott III (Zondervan, 1995).

Every couple has a restless aching, not just to know God individually but to experience God together. But how do you really allow God to fill the soul of your marriage? This book gives you a road map for cultivating rich spiritual intimacy in your relationship by providing fifty-two practical weekly devotions to help you and your partner cross the hurdles of marriage to grow closer than you've ever imagined. It also contains insights from real-life soul mates like Tony and Peggy Campolo, Bill and Vonette Bright, and dozens of others.

Chapter Thirteen:
Questions About Being a Team

More than anything we want to have a wonderful marriage. We are both committed and faithful, but is that the most important quality of a successful marriage?

Traveling through a small town, we once ate in a restaurant where a percentage discount was given for every year a couple celebrating a wedding anniversary had been married. The restaurant manager had taken pictures of anniversary couples and posted them under a sign which read "Successful Marriages." We weren't celebrating our anniversary that day, but it got us thinking about what it means to have a "successful marriage." At what point can a marriage be classified as such? Should we consider a marriage successful just because it has lasted twenty-five, or thirty, or even fifty years?

Those who do research on marriage make a critical distinction between marital quality and marital success.[1] Success is traditionally measured in years while marital quality is defined as how good the marriage is according to the spouses. Marriages in which partners say they are happy and satisfied are judged to be of higher quality than those that aren't. So it is possible that a marriage can last until the old-age death of one spouse and be classified as a "successful" marriage, but that does not ensure that it was one of quality.

You might be interested to know that researchers have found that how spouses deal with one another after marriage is more important to marital quality than the background characteristics they had going into marriage. In other words, marriages between people of similar socioeconomic or ethnic backgrounds are no more or less likely to be of high quality than marriages between people from dissimilar social backgrounds. One of the most important characteristics of not only a successful marriage but also a quality marriage is that the couple develops as a team, sharing personal traits, holding common values, sharing leisure activities, having joint friends, and sharing participation in decision making.[2]

Since marital quality is a measure of marital satisfaction at one point in time, it may fluctuate over the course of the marriage. The effect on marital quality of employment patterns, pregnancy, parenthood, and aging influences how couples rate their happiness. The point is that as you are becoming a team in marriage, you set your goals not only on going the distance, but on enjoying the ride too.

We've worked hard to share everything equally as husband and wife. We split household chores, we divvy up our money, and so on. If one of us buys new clothes, then the other is next. We have been married almost two years now, however, and our fifty-fifty plan is not holding up. Any suggestions?

Scorekeeping is for athletic contests, not marriages. Yet many couples decide that marriage should be a fifty-fifty proposition, and they fall into the habit of tallying up each other's contributions to the marriage. They split resources, weigh portions, and count privileges. They erroneously believe that keeping track of who gets what, does what, and has what can help them achieve a more equal share in the costs and the benefits of running a home.

The truth is that scorekeeping destroys emotional intimacy because it is a subtle way of drawing marital battle lines. You may decide at the outset to have a fifty-fifty marriage because you want to be equal in all things. But you will end up being unhappy marital accountants who are more concerned that you haven't gotten ripped off than that your marriage is growing. Instead of "sweet nothings," you will begin to hear statements like "You got to choose last time," "It's only fair that . . .," and "I thought we had a deal." These are not the sounds of a loving marriage. The longer this fifty-fifty game is played, the more complex it gets, too. As you go along, each of you will discover different expectations, and each of you will measure contributions by different standards.

Regardless of how it gets started, scorekeeping in marriage generally isn't just a division of labor; it's about power, feeling loved and appreciated, and other emotional issues. When marriage is built on a fifty-fifty proposition, both partners eventually feel that they are getting cheated out of their presumed rights for their portions, their privileges. It is far better to give one another the benefit of the doubt when you can and also talk openly about what you are feeling and needing. If you feel like your spouse is spending more money on clothes than you are, talk about it. There may be a pretty good reason for that expense. And if there isn't, your discussion can serve as the impetus for reining it in. The point is that you can build a happier marriage by putting away your scorecards and talking about your feelings and needs.

So do what you can to break the fifty-fifty proposition. Begin by having a calm, frank discussion about expectations and disappointments. Talk about how each of you is tempted to keep score. Be sure to cover the issues where you are most likely to keep score. Be honest about your feelings so that your spouse knows what matters most to you. Next, release your desire to have all your needs met by your spouse. It isn't possible. No person can meet all of your needs, no matter how strategic, compromising, or egalitarian. Ultimately, you can only get your needs met in God. So work on subordinating your needs to your spouse's needs instead of looking out for number one. It's the best way to build a team.

Only you can set the criteria for what is important to you in your marriage. You may see other couples who measure everything in equitable terms, but don't let that influence your desire to work as one. As we said in our book *Saving Your Marriage Before It Starts*, a fifty-fifty marriage only works if each partner is a fraction. And of course, we aren't.

When it comes to being a team as husband and wife, we struggle with the biblical principle of submission and headship. In fact, it has caused a great deal of tension in our relationship. How should we handle this principle?

Like many of the Christian couples we have counseled over the years, we try to build our marriage on biblical principles. As seminary graduates, we work diligently at understanding God's Word and how it relates to our marriage. As we do this, there is probably no other verse that we have worked harder to understand, practice, and explain than Ephesians 5:23: "The husband is the head of the wife as Christ is the head of the church, his body, of which he is the Savior."

We have met many sincere men who interpret this statement to mean literally that it is their job to be the boss of their wives. And that it is her job to be submissive to his demands. Of course, nothing could be further from the truth.

Let's start with the word *submit*. It simply means to subordinate yourself to those considered worthy of respect. It means to affirm that others are valued and important enough to be heard, loved, and their needs responded to. This is a biblical principle that applies to *all* of us—not exclusively to wives. If we take seriously verses like Romans 12:10 ("honor one another above yourselves") and Philippians 2:3 ("in humility consider others better than yourselves"), we would not get hung up on this verse in Ephesians 5. All of us are called to submit, not only wives to husbands, but husbands to wives.

In the Bible the husband is never called to make his wife submit. The Bible doesn't call husbands to rule over their wives but to renounce their desire to be master. Out of reverence for

Christ, husbands should be the first to honor and respect their wives. That's what is meant by "headship." Headship is not being the first in line. It is not being the boss or ruler. It is being the first to honor, the first to nurture, the first to meet your partner's needs.

A healthy marriage is built on a mutual desire to subordinate one's needs to the other. As Ephesians 5:21 says: "Submit to one another out of reverence for Christ." That's the basic principle. Emptying ourselves of our self-centered desires is the bridge to becoming one in marriage. Without mutual submission every marriage, no matter how romantic, will eventually falter. As Amos 3:3 says, "Do two walk together unless they have agreed to do so?"

Paul said it quite plainly. Husbands are to be the heads of their wives "as Christ is the head of the church (Ephesians 5:23). Paul then explains that Christ "loved the church and gave himself up for her to make her holy" (vv. 25–26). Headship to Christ didn't mean domination. It meant self-sacrifice. Headship didn't mean "I'm the boss." It meant "How can I meet your needs?" For the Christian husband, headship means putting his wife's needs before his own. It means doing everything he can to help her reach her full potential as a person and as a Christian. It means loving and self-sacrificing, as Christ did.

Think of it this way. The wife sets the example of submission by placing the needs of the marriage above her personal needs. The husband sets the example of loving by placing the needs of his wife above his own. Each makes it easier for the other by taking the lead in his or her own unique contribution to the Christian marriage.

If we worry about our partner submitting to us, by the way, we have not grasped this important principle. The key is seeing that submission is a two-way street in marriage. Scripture not only calls husbands and wives to "submit to one another" (Ephesians 5:21), but we are to also submit to God (Hebrews 12:9; James 4:7).

I purchased an entertainment center for our family room and thought my wife would be thrilled. She wasn't. I told her about the good price I got, but she still complained about me making a decision to spend that kind of money without her. I didn't think it was a big deal, but she did. How do I know when a decision needs to be made by both of us?

Every couple faces important turning points, critical times when a decision will steer them in new directions. The decision may involve having children, changing careers, relocating, buying a home, and on and on. These important turning points cannot afford to be taken lightly. Nor can they, in our opinion, afford to be made solo. Not all decisions are important, but when they are, both partners need to have a significant say in what to do.

This, of course, begs the question of what is important and what isn't. At the risk of oversimplifying it, an important decision involves any change that will directly or indirectly affect both of your lives. It's really common sense. Little decisions that have few ramifications do not require a marital summit meeting to determine the outcome, but big decisions that affect your lives beyond the immediate do.

If you are in fact dealing with an important decision, the key is to make careful plans concerning it. You see, too many people make big decisions based on intuition, emotion, or small bits of information. Strategic decision makers have a better strategy.

When an effective couple comes together to decide their future on an important issue, they have a mini-forum where each of them weighs the costs and rewards of whatever they are considering. Literally, they make a list of the positives and then a list of the negatives, putting them all out in the open so that neither has to read the other's mind. They take their time considering the alternatives together. They gather information from several sources. These couples also place a high value on the consideration of personal feelings about the various options as well as the opinions of experts and loved ones.

On top of these proven decision-making principles, the effective couple also avails themselves of divine guidance. They pray together and on their own about how God might lead them in their important decisions. Garry Friesen, coauthor of *Decision Making and the Will of God*, puts forth some foundational principles when discerning God's will on a decision.[3] First, a couple must explore God's Word to discover biblical principles that may be relevant to their decision. Second, in those areas where the Bible gives no specific principles, the couple must take care to choose a course of action that is in harmony with the tenor of Scripture. Third, the couple must humbly submit to the out-working of God's will as it touches each decision.

God's will is not a mystical unknown beyond the comprehension of Christians. God gave us our minds and talents, which he expects us to use. He has given us our life experiences, which are the teachers of the soul. He has given us the Scriptures, which are our fundamental guide for service, attitudes, and relationships, as well as salvation. And God has given us guidance through others who are objective, wise, and caring and who can guide us in making important decisions.

So when you and your partner are faced with a big decision, do not neglect the God-given resources he makes available. And also, do not neglect each other's input. The counsel you receive from your partner is critically important to making a wise decision. As you seek the Lord's will together, you will not only find the best alternative, you will strengthen your marriage in the process.

My husband gets upset when I talk to my best friend about a fight we recently had. I understand how this could make him feel betrayed if I was doing it to hurt him, but I am just very close to my friend and we talk about everything. Is that wrong?

One of the biggest mistakes we see couples making quietly sabotages their capacity to be a team together. It has to do with talking to others—friends, relatives, in-laws—about their partner's flaws and foibles. A wife may, for example, confidentially spill the details of last night's fight to her friend who "promises" to keep it a secret. Or a husband might secretly tell his father about how his wife ran up a huge bill on a credit card. Although such little disclosures may seem relatively harmless at the time, they can actually hurt a marriage.

Loyalty is built on being true. It is built on earning another's confidence. When you become a telltale spouse, you lose loyalty. You fracture any confidence your spouse has in you.

Are we saying never talk to others about your marriage or your partner? Absolutely not. But we are saying watch what you say. For example, it can be healthy and good to talk with a trusted and supportive friend about marital struggles as long as you are not disclosing information that would embarrass your spouse. If he doesn't want others to know he locked himself out of the car and that was the source of a marital blowup, keep that information to yourself. But if you are feeling frustrated in not knowing how to respond to these kinds of situations, you might express this to a friend to gain some objectivity. In doing so, you are not unduly embarrassing your partner and you are not complaining about his behavior.

When you focus on your feelings to others, not your complaints, you are more likely to stay clear of the danger zone. "I feel so helpless when he gets upset at himself" carries a very different tone than "I can't believe how stupid he can be sometimes." It may seem like a fine line, but the messages are very different. The first conveys a desire to process your thoughts and feelings while the latter message conveys a desire to gossip and whine.

It basically comes down to knowing the difference between seeking support and help from somebody outside the relationship versus venting your feelings because you are complaining.

And venting is almost always unhealthy for your marriage and damaging to your sense of loyalty to each other. If you find yourself wanting to vent, that's a pretty clear sign that you should only be talking to your spouse about it. And if you do, your loyalty toward one another will stay intact and even grow.

We each have our own idea about who should do what around the house and are having a difficult time coming to a mutual agreement. Do you have any suggestions on how to best assign household chores?

This is a good question, but it does not lend itself to a universal answer. Every couple carves out their own pattern for taking care of household chores. Through the years, we have tested and tried many varying scenarios and, for the time being, have a pattern that works—in great part because we are aware of some typical pitfalls.

Couples today should be aware of an interesting phenomenon about how they typically handle household chores. Husbands are doing more housework today than they ever have. But that news is not nearly as good as it sounds. As it turns out, husbands believe they are doing a large share of the housework, but they are rarely taking as much responsibility for it as their wives do. A husband, for example, may take out the garbage (two minutes) while the wife does the dishes (fifteen minutes). On average, husbands spend between four and six hours per week doing housework, which represents a relatively small percentage of the total amount of time that is spent in housework. What's even more surprising is that this is based on couples where both the husband and the wife hold full-time jobs.

Believe it or not, wives who work outside the home do about twice as much housework as their husbands.[4] So in a sense, many wives end up doing two jobs, one outside the home and one inside. Their leisure time, compared to their husband's, is greatly reduced. Time becomes their most precious commodity, especially spending more time with their husbands.[5]

Distribution of housework is a critical issue for dual-worker marriages. Surprisingly, many couples remain happy in spite of the wife bearing most of the household responsibilities. For a variety of reasons, the perception by the spouses of the amount of household chores is more important to marital satisfaction than the actual amount of work accomplished by both partners. However, if you are frustrated with your current system and are looking for a new approach, you might begin by making a list of all the chores that need to be done in your home. Make a separate list for daily, weekly, and monthly jobs. Then note the approximate time of each job and finally who does what. This will give you a graphic picture of what is going on. At this point, the two of you should start at ground zero and negotiate your new assignments for a more pleasing distribution. In the process, take into account each other's desires. If one of you would rather vacuum and dust than do the laundry, speak up and say so. The goal is to make it better for both of you.

Let's face it. Chores aren't fun. And unless you have the luxury of affording outside help, you have to find a way of making household activities as painless as possible. Don't put this off; the longer you wait to renegotiate your assignments, the more entrenched your roles will become and the less likely you are to change them. Happy housecleaning.

What are some of the most helpful resources on becoming a team in marriage?

The Marriage Builder by Larry Crabb (Zondervan, 1992).

> This book cuts to the heart of the biblical view of becoming "one flesh" in marriage. Crabb argues convincingly that the deepest needs of human personality—security and significance—ultimately cannot be

satisfied by a marriage partner. We need to turn to the Lord, rather than our spouse, to satisfy our needs. This frees both partners for "soul oneness," a commitment to minister to our spouse's needs rather than manipulating them to meet our own needs. This book is outstanding, and we recommend it to any couple wanting to build a fulfilling team-based marriage.

He Wins, She Wins: Turn the Battle for Control in Your Marriage Into a "Win-Win" Partnership by Glenn P. Zaepefel (Thomas Nelson, 1994).

This book explores a common battle in marriage between the "power partner" and the "passive partner." These styles may be different and the genders may interchange, but the power games between them are always played the same. If you are feeling the pain of the power-passive struggle in your marriage, this book can help bring your relationship to healing and health. It defines the psychological and spiritual hurdles for both partners and offers specific strategies for overcoming the damaging dynamic.

Who's on Top, Who's on Bottom: How Couples Can Learn to Share Power by Robert Schwebel (Newmarket, 1994).

This book is built on the premise that if spouses are to work together as a successful team, they will have to transcend the dominant mode for relationships in our culture: competition. Dr. Schwebel presents the cases of eleven couples, nine of whom successfully learn to master the skills of communication and negotiation and build strong, loving relationships. He describes methods for discussing dissatisfaction, expressing resentments, developing calmness, and what to do when cooperation and negotiation fail. This book, however, is not a manual of steps to happiness. It is more about developing an outlook, an attitude, and a vision to guide your marriage.

CHAPTER FOURTEEN:
QUESTIONS
ABOUT GETTING HELP

Sometimes it feels like we aren't doing very well as a couple, but I'm not sure how we compare to others. How do we know if we ever need professional help?

The ideal of marriage concludes with "and they lived happily ever after." In other words, once you find the right person, fall in love, and marry, all your problems will be over. Of course, this is a fairy tale. In real life, all married couples face problems. But how do you know if your problems are serious enough to get professional help?

There is no clear-cut answer to this question, but a good rule of thumb is that if you are bumping your heads up against the same troubling issue over and over after trying on your own to change it, you can probably benefit from seeing an objective professional counselor or a minister with expertise in marital issues. Whether your struggles center around communication, in-laws, intimacy, money, sexuality, spiritual matters, or conflict in general, a trained professional can help save you years of frustration and lead you to a more fulfilling marriage.

Of course, marriage counselors can also be a tremendous help for couples who are simply wanting to enrich their relationship. You don't have to be struggling or be in a crisis to seek the help of a counselor. Since most of us have never learned how to relate intimately to another, there are many benefits to be derived from discovering what marriage is all about from a trained professional.

Some couples get into trouble because they believe that they can't do much to improve their marriage or they simply don't take the time to find the kind of help they need. Don't fall into this trap. There are too many good resources and counselors out there to not get the help you need. Recognizing that you may not be able to solve a problem on your own is a sign of health and maturity, not inferiority or weakness.

I have read several books on building a successful marriage, and my husband likes me to tell him what I am learning. However, he doesn't like to read. What other ways of learning about marriage are there that both of us might benefit from?

While we cannot hope to do justice to the many ways in which married couples can get help, here is a brief look at some typical avenues.

Marriage counseling is perhaps the most traditional and well-known way in which couples get help. This is typically done by a licensed clinical psychologist or counselor who specializes in marital problems.

Courses on marriage can be found at nearly any local college or university. And while many of these courses take a sociological perspective on marital trends, many schools offer more specialized courses, often in the evening, on marital communication, economics of marriage, and so on.

Couples groups are sometimes organized by a counseling agency. They are designed to help couples become more authentic by discussing issues with other couples in similar predicaments. Some of these groups can become quite emotional when people take off their marital masks.

Marriage enrichment weekends provide a retreat setting where couples work together to improve their marriages. These are typically very experiential, without much lecturing. Instead, couples do interactive exercises that stimulate productive discussions.

Communication workshops are often offered by local counseling centers. These ongoing or weekend workshops use traditional instruction with role-playing exercises to teach couples how to communicate more effectively. An important aspect of a workshop is the group critique where other couples give you feedback on how you are doing during an exercise.

Sex therapy is provided by licensed counselors who focus on a couple's sexual relationship, helping them overcome sexual problems. The therapy is conducted in the traditional way of talking with a counselor about the problem, and the therapist typically provides the couple with exercises to do in their own home.

Marriage seminars are an easy and affordable way of getting a marital boost. Many larger churches sponsor such seminars yearly, and featured marriage experts often provide practical and inspirational information to help you.

Both of us care about our marriage very much and want to do everything we can to make it go the distance. We are experiencing some turbulent water right now and have decided to get professional help to make it through. How can we find a competent counselor?

Unfortunately, the large demand for marriage improvement programs has brought some untrained and unscrupulous people into the field of marriage counseling. However, there are several things you can do to ensure competent help.

To begin with, one of the best places to start is with a good referral. This can come from a physician, minister, nurse, teacher, or even a trusted friend.

Whenever you seek help, it is a good idea to check credentials. The foremost organization in the nation for accrediting and certifying marriage counselors is the American Association of Marriage and Family Therapists, 1717 K Street N.W. #407, Washington, D.C. 20006. At no charge it will supply a list of three or more accredited marriage counselors in your area. Membership in the American Psychological Association (APA) indicates that the person has met minimum training requirements and has agreed to abide by a strict set of ethics in client relationships. Your local phone book usually lists members of the national and/or state psychological associations. The American Association of Sex Educators and Counselors has established certification standards for sex therapists. You can receive a copy of these standards and a list of certified sex therapists by writing to Sex Therapy Certification Committee, American Association of Sex Educators, Counselors, and Therapists, 11 Dupont Circle, Suite 220, Washington, D.C. 20036.

Each of the secular professional organizations mentioned in the above paragraph can be a good source of information, but they are in no way the last word on whether a particular counselor or therapist is competent. And if you are looking for only Christian counselors, these organizations are not going to identify them for you. We recommend several different sources for finding competent Christian counselors. One of the most comprehensive referral lists of Christian counselors is maintained by Focus on the Family in Colorado Springs. If you phone their counseling office at 719–531–3400 they can provide you with several Christian counselors' names and numbers in your area. In addition to a referral from Focus on the Family, you might also want to see if the counselor you are considering is a member of the American Association of Christian Counselors or the Christian Association of Psychological Studies.

Once you have two or three good referrals, the next step is to find out which therapist in your area is the best match for your situation. The best way of doing this is by having a preliminary phone conversation with the counselor. Some questions to ask include:

- Are you certified or licensed?
- Do you work with married couples on a regular basis?
- What are your credentials (degrees)?
- At what university did you earn your degrees?
- What professional associations do you belong to?
- How will you approach our particular issue?
- How many sessions do you expect to see us?

If the phone interview sounds promising, an in-person interview can be scheduled to more accurately determine if a number of sessions would be helpful. Both you and your partner will need to feel comfortable working with the counselor, and in the end you will have to follow your instincts together.

We are interested in workshops or seminar programs that can help us get back on track. What couples' programs have a good track record?

Not every marital struggle requires the help of a therapist or counselor. There are, in fact, weekend programs that have helped thousands of couples strengthen their marriage through different means.

One of the most popular of these programs is "Marriage Encounter." It is also one of the earliest programs designed to help couples improve their marriage. Started by a Catholic priest, Fr. Gabriel Calvo, in 1968, the movement has broadened to include a wide variety of denominations and over one million couples have participated. It has a long history of success in helping people build stronger, more successful relationships. Research indicates that eight or nine of every ten couples who attend a Marriage

Encounter weekend report significant success with it.[1] To learn more about Marriage Encounter, call 1–800–795–LOVE.

Another helpful weekend program is Marriage Enrichment, which has now grown to more than ten thousand couples a year. You may contact Marriage Enrichment at 1–800–634–8325. Also, "Family Life Conferences" are run by Campus Crusade for Christ and are very popular, with more than twenty thousand couples attending annually. Phone this ministry at 501–223–8663.

For deeply troubled marriages, Retrouvaille (ret-troo-vi, French for "rediscovery") is a ministry patterned on Marriage Encounter. In this program couples experience a new technique of communication over a weekend and in follow-up sessions. The communication takes place in three steps repeated many times. First, there are presentations by a pastor and three lead couples who share stories of near-failure of their own marriages. Second, couples are asked to write their answers to questions from the lead couples. And third, couples then read each other's responses and dialogue about the feelings in total privacy. At no time are couples asked to share their problems with anyone else. The twelve follow-up sessions are designed to continue the renewal that begins on the first weekend. To locate a Retrouvaille, call 817–284–7078.

What are some of the most helpful resources on finding the help we need for our marriage?

Marriage Savers: Helping Your Friends and Family Stay Married by Michael J. McManus (Zondervan, 1993).

This excellent resource is dedicated to making divorce extinct. The author outlines several strategies anyone can use to help a friend or loved one stay married. Its uniqueness is that it helps those with strong marriages point their friends and relatives with troubled marriages toward resources that will help them stay married. The book is a storehouse of useful information that has been proven to help marriages make it through tough times.

How to Find the Help You Need by Archibald Hart and Timothy Hogan (Grand Rapids: Zondervan, 1996).

This little book is a gold mine for finding a reputable counselor who can help you in your marriage. The authors know the pitfalls involved in finding qualified help, and they answer common concerns in plain language. They offer insights into saving time and money in counseling, red flags to watch for in a counselor, the kinds of help available, and so on. *How to Find the Help You Need* will point you to the right path for hope, healing, and growth.

NOTES

Chapter One: Questions About Communication

1. Larry Barker, Karen Gladney, Renee Edwards, Frances Holley, and Connie Gaines, "An Investigation of Proportional Time Spent in Various Communication Activities by College Students," *Journal of Applied Communications Research* 8 (1980): 101–109.

2. Robert and Rosemary Barnes, *Rock-Solid Marriage: Building a Permanent Relationship in a Throw-Away World* (Grand Rapids: Zondervan, 1996).

3. Albert Mehrabain, *Silent Messages: Implicit Communication of Emotions and Attitudes* (Belmont, CA: Wadsworth, 1981).

4. John Gottman, *Why Marriages Succeed or Fail* (New York: Simon & Schuster, 1994).

5. R. M. Sabatelli, R. Buck, and A. Dreyer, "Nonverbal Communication Accuracy in Married Couples: Relationship with Marital Complaints," *Journal of Personality and Social Psychology* 43, no. 5 (1982): 1088–97.

Chapter Two: Questions About Conflict

1. John Gottman, *Why Marriages Succeed or Fail* (New York: Simon & Schuster, 1994).

2. Diane Vaughan, *Uncoupling: How Relationships Come Apart* (New York: Vintage Books, 1986).

Chapter Three: Questions About Careers

1. S. Lewis, D. Izraelie, and H. Hootsman, eds., *Dual-Earner Families* (Newbury Park, CA: Sage Publications, 1992).

2. William Johnson and Jonathan Skinner, *American Economic Review* 76, no. 3 (1986). Quoted in "Working Women and Divorce: Cause or Effect," *Psychology Today* (October 1986): 12–13.

3. S. Scarr, D. Phillips, and K. McCartney, "Working Mothers and Their Families," *American Psychologist* (November 1989): 1402–9.

4. U.S. Bureau of the Census, January 1993.

5. Arlie Hochschild, *The Second Shift* (New York: Viking, 1989).

6. B. Glassner, *Career Crash: America's New Crisis and Who Survives* (New York: Simon & Schuster, 1994), 16.

7. H. Maurer, *Not Working: An Oral History of the Unemployed* (New York: Holt, Reinhart & Winston, 1979), 5.

8. L. Dumas, "You're Fired," *Health* 20 (July 1988): 38–40, 74.

Chapter Four: Questions About Emotions

1. Douglas McMurry and Everett L. Worthington, Jr., *Value Your Mate* (Grand Rapids: Baker, 1993).

2. Jerry Adler, "Hey, I'm Terrific!" *Newsweek* (February 17, 1992): 46–51.

3. Dennis and Barbara Rainey, *Building Your Mate's Self-Esteem* (Nashville: Thomas Nelson, 1993).

4. David Mace, *Love and Anger in Marriage* (Grand Rapids: Zondervan, 1982).

5. Neil Clark Warren, *Make Anger Your Ally* (New York: Doubleday, 1983).

6. David Mace, *Love and Anger in Marriage*.

7. Lee Robins and Darrell Regier, *Psychiatric Disorders in America: The Epidemiologic Catchment Area Study* (New York: Free Press, 1991), 72.

8. Gary and Julie Collins, "Dealing with Depression," in *Husbands and Wives* (Wheaton, IL: Victor Books, 1988).

9. Archibald D. Hart, *Depression: Coping and Caring* (Arcadia, CA: Cope Publications, 1981).

10. Les Parrott III, *Love's Unseen Enemy: How to Overcome Guilt to Build Healthy Relationships* (Grand Rapids: Zondervan, 1994).

11. S. Bruce Narramore, *No Condemnation: Rethinking Guilt Motivation in Counseling, Preaching, and Parenting* (Grand Rapids: Zondervan, 1984).

12. Henry Nouwen, *Reaching Out* (Garden City, NY: Doubleday, 1975).

Chapter Five: Questions About Gender

1. Willard F. Harley, *His Needs, Her Needs* (Grand Rapids: Fleming H. Revell, 1986).

2. Deborah Tannen, *You Just Don't Understand: Women and Men in Conversation* (New York: Ballantine, 1990).

Chapter Six: Questions About In-laws

1. Jean Parvin, "Do Your In-Laws Drive You Crazy?" *Reader's Digest* (June 1994): 165–70.

Chapter Seven: Questions About Intimacy

1. Lillian Rubin, *Intimate Strangers: Men and Women Together* (New York: Harper & Row, 1983), 90.

2. R. S. Miller and H. M. Lefcourt, "The Assessment of Social Intimacy," *Journal of Personality Assessment* 46 (1982): 514–18.

3. John Gottman, *Why Marriages Succeed or Fail* (New York: Simon & Schuster, 1994).

4. H. Norman Wright, *Holding On to Romance* (Ventura, CA: Regal, 1992), 27.

5. Howard J. Clinebell, Jr. and Charlotte H. Clinebell, *The Intimate Marriage* (San Francisco: Harper & Row, 1970), 37–38.

6. S. T. Ortega, "Religious Homogamy and Marital Happiness," *Journal of Family Issues* 2 (1988): 224–39.

7. Helen Fisher, *Anatomy of Love* (New York: W. W. Norton, 1992).

Chapter Eight: Questions About Money

1. Larry Burkett, *Debt-Free Living: How to Get Out of Debt (And Stay Out)* (Chicago: Moody Press, 1989).

2. P. Blumstein and P. Schwartz, *American Couples: Money, Work, and Sex* (New York: William Morrow, 1983).

3. Martin Zweig, *Winning on Wall Street* (New York: Warner Books, 1990).

Chapter Ten: Questions About Personality

1. David Keirsey and Marilyn Bates, *Please Understand Me: Character & Temperament Types* (Del Mar, CA: Prometheus Nemesis, 1984), 67.

2. Kevin Leman, *Were You Born for Each Other?* (New York: Delacorte, 1991), 23.

3. Bill Hybels, *Honest to God?* (Grand Rapids: Zondervan, 1990), 68–69.

Chapter Eleven: Questions About Sex

1. R. J. Levine and A. Levine, "Sexual Pleasure: The Surprising Preferences of 100,000 Women," *Redbook* (September 1975): 51–58.

2. P. Blumstein and P. Schwartz, *American Couples: Money, Work, and Sex* (New York: William Morrow, 1983).

3. C. Tavris and S. Sadd, *The Redbook Report on Female Sexuality* (New York: Delacorte, 1977).

4. C. Rubenstein and C. Tavris, "Special Survey Results: 26,000 Women Reveal the Secrets of Intimacy," *Redbook* (September 1987): 147–49, 214, 216.

5. Blumstein and Schwartz, *American Couples: Money, Work, and Sex*.

6. C. S. Greenblat, "The Salience of Sexuality in the Early Years of Marriage," *Journal of Marriage and the Family* 45 (1983): 298–99.

7. Ibid.

8. C. Tavris and S. Sadd, *The Redbook Report on Female Sexuality* (New York: Delacorte, 1977).

9. Sources: J. Seligman, "A Condom for Women Moves One Step Closer to Reality," *Newsweek* (February 10, 1992): 45; S. Findlay, "Birth Control," *U.S. News & World Report* (December 24, 1990): 58–64; J. S. Hyde, *Understanding Human Sexuality*, 4th ed. (New York: McGraw-Hill, 1990).

10. E. Rank, C. Anderson, and D. Rubinstein, "Frequency of Sexual Dysfunction in 'Normal' Couples," *New England Journal of Medicine* 229 (1978): 111–15.

11. I. P. Spector and M. P. Carey, "Incidence and Prevalence of the Sexual Dysfunctions: A Critical Review of the Empirical Literature," *Archives of Sexual Behavior* 19 (1990): 389–408.

12. J. A. McFalls, Jr., "The Risks of Reproductive Impairment in the Later Years of Childbearing," *Annual Review of Sociology* 16 (1990): 491–519.

13. R. Segraves, "Effects of Psychotropic Drugs on Human Erection and Ejaculation," *Archives of General Psychiatry* 46 (1989): 275–84;. G. Wyatt, S. Peters, and D. Guthrie Kinsey, "Comparisons of the Sexual Socialization and Sexual Behavior of White Women Over 33 Years," *Archives of Sexual Behavior* 17 (1988): 201–39.

14. Henry Virkler, *Broken Promises: Understanding, Healing, and Preventing Affairs in Christian Marriages* (Dallas: Word, 1992).

15. Charles Mylander, *Running the Red Lights: Putting the Brakes on Sexual Temptation* (Ventura, CA: Regal, 1986): 42.

16. Douglas Rosenau, *A Celebration of Sex: A Christian Couple's Manual* (Nashville: Thomas Nelson, 1994), 317.

17. L. Feinauer, "Relationship of Long-term Effects of Childhood Sexual Abuse to Identity of the Offender: Family, Friend, or Stranger," *Women and Therapy* 7 (1988): 89–107.

18. J. Golden, "A Second Look at a Case of Inhibited Sexual Desire," *Journal of Sex Research* 25 (1988): 304–306.

Chapter Twelve: Questions About Spiritual Matters

1. R. L. Gorsuch, "Measurement: The Boom and Bane of Investigating Religion," *American Psychologist* 39 (1984): 228–36.

2. Jo Berry, *Beloved Unbeliever: Loving Your Husband into the Faith* (Grand Rapids: Zondervan, 1981).

Chapter Thirteen: Questions About Being a Team

1. N. D. Glenn, "Quantitative Research on Marital Quality in the 1980s: A Critical Review," *Journal of Marriage and the Family* 52 (1990): 818–31.

2. M. K. Whyte, *Dating, Mating, and Marriage* (New York: Aldine de Gruyter, 1990).

3. G. Friesen and J. R. Robinson, *Decison Making and the Will of God: A Biblical Alternative to the Traditional View* (Portland, OR: Multnomah, 1980).

4. M. Benin and J. Agostinelli, "Husbands' and Wives' Satisfaction with the Division of Labor," *Journal of Marriage and the Family* 3 (1988): 349–61.

5. D. Blankenhorn, *Rebuilding the Nest: A New Commitment to the American Family* (Milwaukee: Family Service America, 1990).

Chapter Fourteen: Questions About Getting Help

1. A 1990 study, called "Worldwide Marriage Encounter: National Survey and Assessment," was conducted by the National Institute for the Family (3019 Fourth St., N.E., Washington, D.C. 20017).

Becoming Soul Mates

*Cultivating Spiritual Intimacy
in the Early Years of Marriage*

DRS. LES & LESLIE PARROTT III

Becoming Soul Mates gives you a road map for cultivating rich spiritual intimacy in your relationship.
Fifty-two practical weekly devotions help you and
your partner dig deep for a strong spiritual foundation in the early years of marriage.

In each session you will find:

- An insightful devotion that focuses on mar-
  riage-related topics
- A key passage of Scripture
- Questions that will spark discussions on crucial issues
- Insights from real-life soul mates like Pat and Shirley Boone,
  Zig and Jean Ziglar, and Tony and Peggy Campolo
- Questions that will help you and your partner better understand
  each other's unique needs and remember them in prayer during
  the week

Start building on the closeness you've got today—and reap the
rewards of a deep, more satisfying relationship in the years ahead.
Pick up *Becoming Soul Mates* at your local Christian bookstore.

Becoming Soul Mates
0-310-20014-8 Hardcover

ZONDERVAN™

GRAND RAPIDS, MICHIGAN 49530 USA

WWW.ZONDERVAN.COM